Encyclopedia of
Peace Education

Encyclopedia of Peace Education

edited by

Monisha Bajaj
Teachers College, Columbia University

Information Age Publishing, Inc.
Charlotte, North Carolina • www.infoagepub.com

Library of Congress Cataloging-in-Publication Data

Encyclopedia of peace education / edited by Monisha Bajaj.
   p. cm.
  Includes bibliographical references and index.
  ISBN 978-1-59311-898-3 (pbk.) -- ISBN 978-1-59311-899-0 (hardcover) 1. Peace--Study
and teaching--Encyclopedias. I. Bajaj, Monisha.
  JZ5534.E48 2008
  303.6'6071--dc22

                        2008004586

ISBN 13: 978-1-59311-898-3 (pbk.)
         978-1-59311-899-0 (hardcover

Cover art used with permission by UNICEF/HQ92-0617/ I DREAM OF PEACE, FORMER
YUGOSLAVIA   Old Ref # c 115 32, positive IMG0017.PCD "Messages" "Poruke" (Dove with
olive branch amidst flowers) Maja, 12 years-old, from Pozega

CONTENTS

CHAPTER 1

INTRODUCTION

Monisha Bajaj

The Encyclopedia of Peace Education brings together scholars and practitioners with decades of experience in peace education with the aim of tracing developments in the field to date. Although its foundation is rooted in the early nineteenth century, peace education emerged primarily during the post-World War II era, resulting in diverse definitions and constituencies worldwide. This edited volume attempts to explore major issues in the field by giving voice to individuals who have advanced foundational concepts related to peace and education over the past four decades. Additionally, this book seeks to highlight future perspectives of emerging scholars who are shaping the field in new ways. Exploring perspectives on peace education can provide greater clarity as to what the term means and what shared understandings exist, as well as what specificities are open for further analysis and interpretation

Peace education is generally defined as educational policy, planning, pedagogy, and practice that can provide learners—in any setting—with the skills and values to work towards comprehensive peace (Reardon, 1988). Comprehensive peace includes the oft-discussed domains of both "negative" and "positive" peace that, respectively, comprise the abolition of direct or physical violence, and structural violence constituted by systematic inequalities that deprive individuals of their basic human

Encyclopedia of Peace Education, pp. 1–11
Copyright © 2008 by Information Age Publishing
All rights of reproduction in any form reserved.

rights (Galtung, 1969). The areas of human rights education, development education, environmental education, disarmament education, and conflict resolution education are often included in a broader understanding of the multifaceted approaches of peace education. Despite different approaches, the holistic aim of peace education can be summarized as the achievement of "all human rights for all people(s)" (Toh, 2006, p. 15).

While the structural analysis of notions of negative and positive peace is one of the unifying concepts in the field of peace education, other central elements include the beliefs that: (1) the process of education can impart in all students social "goods," in this case, the skills and values needed for peace and social justice; and (2) once given the relevant information and experience, individual students can be agents in promoting local, national, and international peace. This does not mean that all peace educators believe such transformation happens in all cases; rather, many speak of a "possibility" for transformation through education. Beyond these unifying concepts, much diversity exists among the political, theoretical, and methodological orientations of scholars and practitioners involved in peace education worldwide.

Hence, a primary objective of this edited volume is to provide greater nuance to debates around peace education by exploring the range of ideas, perspectives, and conceptualizations that have come to influence the field. This volume provides students, practitioners, and scholars of peace education an introduction to the historical emergence of, foundational concepts in, and disciplinary influences on the field. The glossary in the back of the book is intended to provide approximate definitions of terminology often used by scholars. It is hoped that by engaging with the topics and issues in this book, readers will gain a greater perspective on their own positionality in the field and the debates that exist within it in order to advance both scholarship and practice. The larger historical, social, and conceptual contexts that have given rise to the field of peace education should provide important insights into what binds us together as members of a shared epistemological community— despite our varied orientations and locations within it—and the way(s) forward in the pursuit of greater equity and social justice.

This "primer" in peace education also offers those new to the field the opportunity to engage with scholars who have devoted significant time and attention to developing ideas and strategies for discussing and theorizing peace and peace education. The discussion questions posed at the beginning of each section provide readers the opportunity to engage in meaningful inquiry and dialogue in order to probe some of the key problematiques in peace education. This volume seeks to open avenues for debate, dialogue, and discussion. As such, the authors presented are not deemed authoritative, but rather, represent some of the many key ideas amidst a vast range of those that exist on each topic.

The idea for an *Encyclopedia of Peace Education* emerged as a way to have an ongoing dialogue with scholars and practitioners from around the world in a dynamic way utilizing technology. In compiling entries for an online encyclopedia, some stood out as containing foundational concepts or provocative ideas that seemed useful to concretize and provide to educators, students, and scholars in the form of this edited volume. The topics for this book were chosen because they represented critical points of engagement for those interested in peace education. Readers are encouraged to visit the online encyclopedia as well where, at the time of this writing, some 35 entries on a vast array of topics related to peace education are located (see the Appendix for list).

One of the common elements that unite scholars and practitioners who claim membership in the field of peace education is optimism that education can lead to positive social change. In order to counter the critique that peace education scholars and practitioners exhibit "naiveté" or "blind optimism" (Gur-Ze'ev, 2001, p. 315), it is important to explore the contours of optimism as they pertain to this field.

PEACE EDUCATION: ENVISIONING "TRANSFORMATIVE OPTIMISM" IN RESEARCH AND PRACTICE

One of the founding principles of peace education initiatives is that learners can develop a sense of possibility that enables them to become agents of social change. Freirean ideas on the necessity for educators to inspire a critical optimism among students that is aimed at promoting solidarity and diminishing the distance between social groups—whether they are stratified by race, ethnicity, religion, class, or any other ascriptive characteristic—are particularly relevant for our understanding of peace education. However, the cultivation of hope alone, without a critical understanding of the social conditions that constrain action and diminish optimism among the marginalized, can be, as Freire (1998) contends, counterproductive:

> The idea that hope alone will transform the world, and action undertaken in that kind of naïveté, is an excellent route to hopelessness, pessimism, and fatalism. But the attempt to do without hope, in the struggle to improve the world, as if that struggle could be reduced to calculated acts alone, or a purely scientific approach—is a frivolous illusion. To attempt to do without hope, which is based on the need for truth as an ethical quality of the struggle, is tantamount to denying that struggle of its mainstays. (p. 8)

Peace education aimed at raising learners' critical consciousness (Freire, 1970) must provide students with an accurate understanding of their social and political contexts while simultaneously focusing attention towards possibilities for action and change.

In assessing the movement from the dangerous "blind optimism" towards the preferred "transformative optimism," Freirean scholar Cesar Augusto Rossatto (2005) identifies and maps four categories of optimism. The first category is that of "anti-optimism," or fatalism, where social conditions are understood and believed to provide no hope for mobility or change. The extreme opposite of this fatalist condition is equally at odds with the goals of peace education: blind optimism. Disconnected from social realities and operating in an idyllic cocoon, this type of blind optimism or naïveté results in frustration and disenfranchisement once unequal structures are revealed. For those in positions of privilege or relative advantage, blind optimism can often serve as a placebo for organized collective action toward social change. The challenge implied in Rossatto's critique of this form of optimism is to interrogate and analyze the larger structures of inequality that often lead to direct and structural violence in global contexts.

Rossatto moves from these two unproductive forms of optimism to identify two other categories of optimism at the individual and collective levels. Resilient optimism primarily is found when an individual overcomes obstacles posed by social or political marginalization and achieves upward mobility. However, the likely outcome, rather than a commitment to greater collective action towards social change, is "an assimilationist optimism that reproduces the hegemonic social order" (Rossatto, 2005, p. 69). While assimilating to one's more privileged position in an unjust order is the product of resilient optimism, the author identifies a more beneficial strategy that educators can strive to nurture among students: transformative optimism.

Transformative optimism, which underscores a sense of agency, provides the most comprehensive definition of hope for peace educators. Rossatto (2005) defines transformative optimism as resistance to structural violence in which each individual "sees himself or herself as a necessary and viable participant in the collective process of social change" (p. 81). Solidarity with others in this shared struggle for social change is an essential component to ensure a more just future. Peace educators could certainly utilize Rossatto's notion of transformative optimism as an organizing principle for research and practice.

The goal of highlighting Rossatto's conceptualization of transformative optimism is to provide a framework that does not explicitly define a preferred outcome for what learners will think and do, but to suggest a set of core values for how they will approach the obstacles to peace and respect for human rights in their respective communities and societies. Consciousness-raising and an orientation towards equity and social justice all emerge from the structure, content, and pedagogy of peace education. In this process, attention to the social and political contexts of education is essential such that envisioning a better future does not stifle creative action, but provides an understanding of the constraints of and possibilities for it.

SUMMARY OF CHAPTERS

The chapters included in this book provide an overview of scholarly developments in the field of peace education and innovative ideas for the way ahead. Each section provides readers a concise and engaging glimpse into topics that are timely and relevant in advancing our understanding of peace education. Introductions in every section include a list of questions for further consideration and holistic investigation into the synergistic aspects of the various topics. These questions also serve as a starting point for educators to edit and expand upon for use as a resource in classrooms.

The goal of this volume is to outline the theoretical and conceptual underpinnings of peace education, survey contemporary perspectives, and provide a space for scholars to envision the future of the field. The edited volume includes the following sections, which will be reviewed in more detail below: (1) the historical emergence of and influences on peace education; (2) foundational perspectives in peace education; (3) core concepts in peace education; and (4) frameworks and new directions for peace education.

Section I: The Historical Emergence of and Influences on Peace Education

Noted peace education scholar, Ian Harris, presents an historical account of the growth of peace education. With its early foundations in the world's organized religions, peace education has been practiced informally by generations of people searching for ways to resolve conflicts without violence or deadly force. Peace education continues to be carried out informally in community settings, but there is a recent trend of peace educators unifying around a more formal peace education reliant on the written word, instruction, and common curriculum, and which incorporates its historical roots with modern conventions of human rights and environmental concerns.

In his chapter, Charles F. Howlett makes a link between Dewey's writings and peace education. Dewey's contribution to peace education was based on his view that schools could serve as a basis for dynamic change, and that teaching subjects like history and geography should be premised on the goal of promoting internationalism and international understanding. His educational objective was to counter the philistine notion of patriotism and nationalism developed by individual nation-states which had been a basic cause of war.

Cheryl Duckworth discusses the inherently multidisciplinary nature of peace education, which has led to the ambiguity of its emergence, definition, and boundaries. Famous for her child-centered learning approach, Maria Montessori is identified as a founder of the field, arguing that education is a means of eliminating war. Montessori's methods reinforce the commitment to global citizens who live and work for lasting peace through the fostering of independent critical thinking, imaginative problem solving, and moral values of responsibility and respect. Positive peace education methodologies reflect a harmonization of implicit and explicit curricula to develop the whole child.

Lesley Bartlett describes the impact that the theories of Brazilian education scholar Paulo Freire have had on peace education by integrating his life experiences and his conceptual development of education. His notions of education as a political act, dialogue and critical consciousness, democratic teacher-student relationships, and coconstruction of knowledge inform peace education pedagogy and practice. Freire's philosophy and concept of conscientization provide a link between peace education and social transformation.

Section II: Foundational Perspectives in Peace Education

Seminal peace studies scholar, Johan Galtung, presents suggestions for the form and content of peace education. According to him, significant advances have been made with respect to peace research and action, but they generally fail to bring their findings into schools and universities. There is no one standard for peace education and although it is not the only factor in peace, peace education can raise the level of consciousness to create a world in which people are aware of their basic human rights.

A long-time peace education scholar, Magnus Haavelsrud, focuses on three major components of the educational problematic: the content, method of communication, and organizational structure of the educational program. The choices made about these three components, which are mutually related, prove to be decisive in defining the substance of any educational program in or outside the school, including education for peace. This essay discusses important dimensions within which it is believed the major conceptual disagreements between "peace" and "education" are to be found.

Educational philosopher, Dale Snauwaert, discusses concepts of morality in politics and peace education. He contrasts political realism, which denies the existence of morality in international politics, with peace education, which is premised upon the belief that all human beings have moral standing. Thus, war and peace, and justice and injustice, are global moral considerations. A global moral community is not merely a philosophical ideal, and peace education should therefore aim to transform social consciousness and social structures.

James Page discusses peace education at a global institutional level, mediated by the United Nations (UN) and how its goals are aligned with maintaining international peace and encouraging international co-operation, thereby preventing war. With a long commitment to disarmament education, the United Nation's programs for tolerance and human rights have led to an emphasis on creating a culture of peace. The development of such educational programs stems from an evolving awareness that the attainment of peace is not merely an institutional problem, but rather one that requires the subtle elements of cultural and societal change.

Section III: Core Concepts in Peace Education

A leading figure in educational philosophy, Nel Noddings draws connections between caring theory and peace education, describing the elements of each to highlight their integration. She argues that engaging in continuous dialogue can encourage understanding of intentions and motivations, avoiding the main points of contention on a global scale, and thereby expanding the circles of caring. Noddings offers useful advice for peace educators about the need for intercultural dialogue and reflection.

Carl Mirra defines the multiple forms of militarism using existing literature. He correctly identifies that peace educators paid particular attention to militarism during the Cold War and its attendant arms race. Disarmament education was offered as an alternative to the rising tide of militarism and war preparations. The goal of peace education is to reverse the adverse effects of militarism and redefine human security.

Felisa Tibbitts defines human rights education as an international movement to promote awareness about the rights accorded by the Universal Declaration of Human Rights and related human rights conventions. Although the definition is not specific to the schooling sector, the United Nations proposes human rights education (HRE) for all sectors of society as part of a "lifelong learning" process for individuals. HRE is emerging in the work of nongovernmental organizations at the grassroots level as well as in national systems of education. HRE calls attention to overall school policies, pedagogy, and practices in order to promote greater awareness and internalization of human rights values.

Lynn Davies' chapter examines the nature of global citizenship education and its role in peace education. She discusses the contestation of the definition of global citizenship and the debate over what sort of education prepares someone to be a global citizen. Global education for peace requires knowledge of world events, capacity for critical analysis, political skills, and willingness for joint action to produce active world citizens who understand the causes and effects of conflict.

Section IV: Frameworks and New Directions for Peace Education

Robin Burns, through a comprehensive literature review, highlights the in/compatibility of comparative and international education as a framework for peace education based on the extent of the field, appropriate subject-matter, and methodology. The author then discusses the changes over time in the field, including the inclusion of an ameliorative element to educational planning and systems, the critique of globalization, and how such changes suggest the inclusion of peace education as a legitimate topic for study.

With a discussion of its nine elements, David Hicks argues that a futures perspective is crucial to peace education as it enables learners to think more critically and purposefully to create a preferred future. While peace education is concerned with a wide variety of issues that manifest at scales from the local to the global, such issues cannot be understood without an exploration of the interrelationships between past, present, and future, an often a missing dimension in education.

In my chapter, I argue for a reclaimed "critical peace education" in which research aimed towards local understandings of how participants can cultivate a sense of transformative agency assumes a central role. Attention to research and the renewed pursuit of critical structural analyses can further the field towards scholar-activism in pursuit of peace education's emancipatory promise. Approaches to research and practice in peace education are discussed and suggestions are made for greater attention to the causes and dimensions of social, political, and economic conflicts in their respective settings.

Finally, H. B. Danesh defines unity as the main law governing all human relationships and conflict as the absence of unity. He outlines the integrative theory of peace and a comprehensive unity-based peace education program, Education for Peace, which has been successfully implemented in the postconflict societies of Bosnia and Herzegovina. Because conflict is the absence of unity, conflict resolution, and peace creation are only possible in the context of a unity-based worldview that espouses individual and collective development.

Taken together, the chapters in this volume seek to provide a unified basis for understanding and exploring diverse perspectives in the field of peace education. It is hoped that through this volume, greater clarity will emerge as to *what is peace education* in an attempt to further explore the contours of this evolving field. Far from seeking to create disciplinary gatekeepers, this volume charts the history of peace education, identifies key conceptual streams, and highlights new thinking on the future of the field. Readers are encouraged to actively engage with the material contained in this volume and to, as eminent peace education scholar Betty Reardon (2000) notes, work towards the fulfillment of peace education's promise to "develop [the] reflective and participatory capacities for applying [peace] knowledge to overcoming problems and achieving possibilities" (p. 381).

ACKNOWLEDGEMENTS

This Encyclopedia owes a tremendous debt of gratitude to the Teachers College students who contributed their time, ideas, and energy to the project, especially Belinda Chiu, Radhika Iyengar, and Annie Smiley. Sina Mossayeb and Christina Ryan provided essential support for the Web design of the online version. Additionally, the authors involved contributed a great deal of input and suggestions to guide the edited volume and online encyclopedia.

APPENDIX

Online Encyclopedia of Peace Education Entries as of 2008

Topic	Authors	Author's Affiliation
Addams, Jane & Peace Education	Charles Howlett	Molloy College
Associated Schools & Peace Education	Lynn Davies	University of Birmingham
Bahai Faith & Peace Education	Marie Gervais	University of Alberta
Boulding, Elise & Peace Education	Mary Lee Morrison	Pax Educare, Inc.
Caring & Peace Education	Nel Noddings	Stanford University
Coexistence education	Daniel Bar-Tal	Tel Aviv University
Comparative and International Education & Peace Education	Robin Burns	La Trobe University
Conceptual Perspectives in Peace Education	Magnus Haavelsrud	Norwegian University of Science and Technology
Curti, Merle & Peace Education	Charles Howlett	Molloy College
Dewey, John & Peace Education	Charles Howlett	Molloy College
Environmental Education	Patricia Mische	Antioch College
Ethical & Spiritual foundations of Peace Education	Dale Snauwaert	University of Toledo
Form and Content of PeaceEducation	Johan Galtung	Transcend University
Freire, Paulo & Peace Education	Lesley Bartlett	Teachers College, Columbia University
Futures Education	David Hicks	Bath Spa University
Global Citizenship Education	Lynn Davies	University of Birmingham
Higher Education & Peace Education	Andria Wisler	Teachers College, Columbia University
History of Peace Education	Ian Harris	University of Wisconsin, Milwaukee
Human Rights Education	Felisa Tibbitts	Human Rights Education Associates
International Institute on Peace Education	Tony Jenkins	Teachers College Peace Education Center
Islam & Peace Education	Mustafa Köylü	Ondokuz Mayis University, Turkey
Learning to Live Together	Margaret Sinclair	UNESCO
Montessori, Maria & Peace Education	Cheryl Duckworth	George Mason University
Multicultural Education	Zvi Bekerman	Hebrew University
NonViolence & Peace Education	Barry Gan	St. Bonaventure University
Theory and Praxis	Surya Nath Prasad	Peace Education Programs & Studies, Maharashtra, India
Peace History Society	Charles Howlett	Molloy College
Philosophy of Peace Education	James S. Page	Southern Cross University
Schooling as a Global Problem	Clive Harber	University of Birmingham

Appendix continues on next page.

Towards a Reclaimed Critical Peace Education	Monisha Bajaj	Teachers College, Columbia University
United Nations and Peace Education	James S. Page	Southern Cross University
United States & Peace Education	Aline Stomfay-Stitz	University of North Florida
Unity-Based Peace Education	H. B. Danesh	International Education for Peace Institute
Youth and Peace Building	Roshan Danesh	International Education for Peace Institute

REFERENCES

Freire, P. (1970). *Pedagogy of the oppressed*. New York: Continuum.

Freire, P. (1998). *Pedagogy of hope*. New York: Continuum.

Galtung, J. (1969). Violence, peace, and peace research. *Journal of Peace Research, 6*(3), 167-191.

Gur Ze'ev, I. (2001). Philosophy of peace education in a postmodern era. *Educational Theory, 51*(3), 315-336.

Reardon, B. (1988). *Comprehensive peace education*. New York: Teachers College Press.

Reardon, B. (2000). Peace education: A review and projection. In B. Moon, M. Ben-Peretz, & S. Brown (Eds.), *International companion to education* (pp. 397-425). New York: Routledge.

Rossatto, C. A. (2005). *Engaging Paulo Freire's pedagogy of possibility*. Oxford, England: Rowman & Littlefield.

Toh, S.-H. (2006, May). *Education for sustainable development & the weaving of a culture of peace: complementarities and synergies.* Paper presented at the UNESCO Expert Meeting on Education for Sustainable Development (ESD), Kanchanaburi, Thailand. Retrieved November 2, 2007, from http://www.unescobkk.org/fileadmin/user_upload/esd/documents/workshops/kanchanburi/toh_culture_of_peace.pdf

SECTION I

The Historical Emergence of and Influences on Peace Education

Peace education is colloquially referred to as the intellectual space where "John Dewey, Maria Montessori, and Paulo Freire meet," given their contributions to concepts that have greatly shaped the field. Dewey's focus on active citizenship, Montessori's elaboration of pedagogy for child-led learning, and Freire's radical notions of personal and collective transformation are particularly relevant for peace education. In this section, the historical emergence of peace education is charted alongside the influential contributions of these prominent educational scholars who are not always considered as founding figures in peace education.

The linkages made between education and social responsibility/action by scholars such as Dewey, Montessori, and Freire, as well as founding figures in peace education such as Betty Reardon, Ian Harris, and Johan Galtung, provide the conceptual unity that underscores the field. This section explores ideas that have led to the growth of the field of peace education.

Encyclopedia of Peace Education, pp. 13–14

QUESTIONS TO CONSIDER

- How have educational theories influenced developments in the field of peace education? What have been the specific contributions of John Dewey, Maria Montessori, and Paulo Freire?
- How has peace education developed across different political, social, and cultural contexts? In what ways can the context impact the scope, nature, and dimensions of peace education initiatives?
- What challenges and opportunities does globalization pose for peace education? In what ways do contemporary political, social, and economic relationships among countries and civil society limit or enable the types of education and action advocated for by scholars?

CHAPTER 2

HISTORY OF PEACE EDUCATION

Ian Harris

INTRODUCTION

Throughout history, humans have taught each other conflict resolution techniques to avoid violence. Peace education is the process of teaching people about the threats of violence and strategies for peace. Peace educators try to build consensus about what types of peace strategies can bring maximum benefit to a group.

Peace education activities that attempt to end violence and hostilities can be carried out informally within communities or formally within institutional places of learning, such as schools or colleges. Peace education has been practiced informally by generations of humans who want to resolve conflicts in ways that do not use deadly force. Many indigenous peoples have nonviolent conflict resolution traditions that have been passed down through millennia that help promote peace within their communities. Anthropologists have located on this planet at least 47 relatively peaceful societies (Banta, 1993). Although there are few written records, human beings throughout history have employed community-based peace education strategies to preserve their knowledge

Encyclopedia of Peace Education, pp. 15–23

of conflict resolution tactics that promote their security. More formal peace education relies upon the written word or instruction through schooling institutions.

RELIGIOUS TEACHINGS THAT PROMOTE PEACE

Perhaps the earliest written records of guidelines that teach others about how to achieve peace come through the world's great religions. These religions—following the teachings of leaders such as Buddha, Baha'u'llah, Jesus Christ, Mohammed, Moses, and Lao Tse—have specific scriptures that advance peace. Organized religions promote their own visions of peace, but ironically, some have utilized religion to advocate violence. That the great religions contribute both to war and peace might be seen as indicative of certain ironic and contradictory aspects of human nature that contribute to the great peace dilemma: Why can't human beings who know about peace figure out how to live in peace?

COMMUNITY-BASED PEACE EDUCATION

One of the first Europeans who used the written word to espouse peace education was Comenius (1642/1969), the Czech educator who in the seventeenth century argued that universally-shared knowledge could provide a road to peace. This approach to peace assumes that an understanding of others and shared values will overcome differences that lead to conflict. The ultimate goal of this education was a world in which men and women would live in harmony with acceptance of diverse cultures.

The growth of peace education parallels the growth of peace movements. The modern peace movement against war began in the nineteenth century after the Napoleonic wars when progressive intellectuals and politicians formed serious societies to study the threats of war and propagate arguments against the build-up of armaments. Indigenous peace organizations sprung up in Great Britain, Belgium, and France. The second wave of nineteenth century peace movements was closely associated with working-men's associations and socialist political groupings. The last wave of the nineteenth-century peace movement occurred right before the World War I. Peace organizations were formed in nearly all European nations during these decades, spreading across the United States and the newly formed states of Italy and Germany. As the nineteenth century drew to a close, groups of teachers, students, and university professors formed peace societies to educate the general public about the dangers of war.

At the beginning of the twentieth century, Europeans and Americans formed peace movements to lobby their governments against the saber rattling that eventually led to World War I. Bertha von Suttner, an Austrian who helped convince Alfred Nobel to establish a peace prize, wrote novels against war and organized international peace congresses (Hamann, 1996). These congresses represented the notion that international conflicts should be resolved by mediation and not weapons. The purpose of such congresses was to sway public opinion against military build-ups that presaged the World War I. Public demonstrations were also aimed at ruling elites to get them to adopt more pacifist policies.

In 1912, a school peace league had chapters in nearly every state in the United States that were "promoting through the schools ... the interests of international justice and fraternity" (Scanlon, 1959, p. 214). They had ambitious plans to familiarize over 500,000 teachers with the necessary conditions for peace (Stomfay-Stitz, 1993). In the interbellum period between World Wars I and II, social studies teachers started teaching international relations so that their students would not want to wage war against foreigners. Convinced that schools had encouraged and enabled war by indoctrinating youth into nationalism, peace educators contributed to a progressive education reform where schools were seen as a means to promote social progress by providing students with an awareness of common humanity that helped break down national barriers that lead to war.

Many of the leading peace educators in the early twentieth century were women. Jane Addams (1907), an American woman who won the Nobel Peace Prize in 1931, was urging schools to include immigrant groups. The slogan "peace and bread" was central to her work and articulated a vision that poverty was a cause of war. She felt that educators needed to understand and relate to the struggles of urban America to create a true democratic community. She rejected the traditional curriculum that limited women's educational choices and opportunities, wanting women to work for reforms that ended child labor. She was also active in international campaigns for the League of Nations, established after World War I to create a global forum whereby the nations of the world could prevent future occurrences of war.

At about this same time, an Italian woman by the name of Maria Montessori was traveling through Europe, urging teachers to abandon authoritarian pedagogies, replacing them with a rigid but dynamic curriculum from which students could choose what to study. She reasoned that children who did not automatically follow authoritarian teachers would be inoculated from authoritarian rulers urging them to war. She saw that the construction of peace depended upon an education that would free the child's spirit, promote love for others, and remove blind obedience to authority. Dr. Montessori emphasized that a teacher's method or pedagogy could contribute towards building a peaceful world. Hence, the whole school should reflect the nurturing characteristics of a healthy family (Montessori, 1946/1974).

The horrors of World War II created a new interest in "Education for World Citizenship." Right after that war, Herbert Read (1949) argued for the marriage of art and peace education to produce images that would motivate people to promote peace. Somewhat like his contemporary, Maria Montessori, he argued that humans could use their creative capacities to escape the pitfalls of destructive violence.

FORMAL, SCHOOL-BASED PEACE PROGRAMS

The first academic peace studies program at the college level was established in 1948 at Manchester College, in North Manchester, Indiana, in the United States. Soon thereafter, the field of peace research developed as a "science of peace" in the 1950s to counteract the science of war that had produced so much mass killing. A Manifesto, issued in 1955 by Bertrand Russell and Albert Einstein and signed by other distinguished academics, called upon scientists of all political persuasions to assemble to discuss the threat posed to civilization by the advent of thermonuclear weapons.

In the 1980s, the threat of nuclear war prompted educators all around the world to warn of impending devastation. Three books were published, representing a decade acutely concerned with the threat of nuclear annihilation: *Education for Peace* by Birgit Brocke-Utne (1985) of Norway, *Comprehensive Peace Education* by Betty Reardon (1988) of the United States, and *Peace Education* by Ian Harris (1988), also of the United States. Brocke-Utne pointed out the devastation that masculine aggression—manifested in militarism, war, and domestic violence—wreaks upon all people, young and old. She argued that feminism is the starting point for effective disarmament. Additionally, she pointed out that societies not at war were not necessarily peaceful because they still harbored considerable domestic violence. Reardon argued that the core values of schooling should be care, concern, and commitment, and the key concepts of peace education should be planetary stewardship, global citizenship, and humane relationships. Harris stressed a holistic approach to peace education that could apply to community education, elementary and secondary schools, as well as college classrooms. He also emphasized that a peaceful pedagogy must be integral to any attempt to teach about peace. The key ingredients of such pedagogy are cooperative learning, democratic community, moral sensitivity, and critical thinking.

This expansion of peace education towards the end of the twentieth century points to an important symbiotic relationship between peace movements, peace research, and peace education. Activists have developed strategies to warn people about the dangers of violence, whether it be wars between nations, environmental destruction, the threat of nuclear holocaust, colonial aggression, cultural, domestic, or structural violence. Academics studying these developments further the field of peace research. The activists, hoping to broaden their message, teach others through informal, community-based peace education activities, such as holding forums, publishing newsletters, and sponsoring peace demonstrations. Teachers observing these activities promote peace studies courses and programs in schools and colleges to provide awareness of the challenges of ecological sustainability, war, and peace.

PEACE EDUCATION IN DIFFERENT CONTEXTS

A rich diversity of peace education is promoted by the myriad of contexts in which it is practiced. Because individuals disagree about how to achieve security, there are many different paths to peace that are explained in peace education classes. An Israeli educator has stated that peace education programs take different forms because of the wide variety of conflicts that plague human existence:

> Even though their objectives may be similar, each society will set up a different form of peace education that is dependent upon the issues at large, conditions, and culture, as well as views and creativity of the educators. (Bar-Tal, 2000, p. 35)

Each different form of violence requires a unique form of peace education to address strategies that could resolve its conflicts. Peace education in intense conflicts attempts to demystify enemy images and urges combatants to withdraw from warlike behavior. Peace education in regions of interethnic tension relies upon multiculturalism and awareness about the sufferings of various groups involved in the conflict to promote empathy for the suffering of others and to reduce hostilities. Peace educators in areas free from collective physical violence teach about the causes of domestic and civil violence and try to develop an interest in global issues, the problems of poverty, environmental sustainability, and the power of nonviolence.

Peace educators concerned about the problems of underdevelopment, starvation, poverty, illiteracy, and the lack of human rights seek an understanding of the crises that exist in poorer countries and solutions for the problems of underdevelopment. Peace educators use development studies to provide insights into the various aspects of structural violence, focusing on social institutions with their hierarchies and propensities for dominance and oppression. Such study highlights the problems of structural violence and emphasizes peace-building strategies to improve human communities.

Peace educators in many countries continue to focus on human rights. Interest in human rights comes from attempts during the twentieth century to establish international organizations like the International Criminal Court that address civil, domestic, cultural, and ethnic forms of violence, to bring to justice tyrants who have aggressed against innocent people. Peace educators falling within this tradition are guided by the December 1948 Universal Declaration of Human Rights that provides a statement of values to be pursued in order to achieve economic, social, and political justice.

Various statements about human rights derive from concepts of natural law, a higher set of laws that are universally applicable and that supersede governmental laws. The study of human rights is the study of treaties, global institutions, and domestic and international courts. This approach to peace, known as "peace through justice," rests on the notion that humans have certain inalienable rights that governments should protect. People being persecuted by their governments for political beliefs can appeal to provisions of international law to gain support for their cause. Abuse of rights and the struggle to eliminate that abuse lie at the heart of many violent conflicts. Human rights institutions champion rights against discrimination based upon gender, disability, and sexual orientation.

At the beginning of the 1980s, peace educators became more concerned about civil, domestic, cultural, and ethnic forms of violence, trying to heal some of the wounds of students who have been raised in violent cultures. As such, they began to expand the teaching of conflict resolution in schools. At the beginning of the new millennium, conflict resolution education is one of the fastest growing school reforms in the West. Conflict resolution educators provide basic communications skills necessary for survival in a postmodern world. Here, the focus is upon interpersonal relations and systems that help disputing parties resolve their differences with communication skills. Approximately 10% of schools in the United States have some sort of peer mediation program (Sandy, 2001). Conflict resolution educators teach human relations skills such as anger management, impulse control, emotional awareness, empathy development, assertiveness, and problem solving. Conflict resolution education provides students with peacemaking skills that they can use to manage their interpersonal conflicts, but does not necessarily address the various kinds of civil, cultural, environmental, and global violence that take place outside schools.

One of the goals often formulated for peace education in intractable conflicts like that between Israel and Palestine in the Middle East is to study the conflict from the perceptions of the "enemy" and thereby develop some empathy for them (Salomon, 2002). Because different groups see conflicts from different perspectives, this approach to peace education attempts to legitimize the point of view of the "other." This does not require agreeing with the other side, but rather seeing its perspective as valid, which might lead to a decrease in tension between two conflicting parties. This approach to peace education attempts to build peace by opening people's hearts.

Another peace education thread that developed at the end of the twentieth century is environmental education. Environmentalists see that the greatest threat to modern life is the destruction of our natural habitat, so that in the immortal words of T. S. Eliot (1936), "This is the way the world ends, not with a bang but a whimper" (p. 107). Up to that point, many peace educators throughout the world had focused on the threat of a cataclysmic nuclear exchange between the United States and the former Soviet Union (which collapsed in 1989). Nowadays, environmental educators help young people become aware of the ecological crisis, give them the tools to create environmental sustainability, and teach them to use resources in a renewable way. They argue that the deepest foundations for peaceful existence are rooted in environmental health and sustainability.

Historically, peace educators concerned about the dangers of war have ignored the environmental crisis. With the rise of global warming, rapid species extinction, water shortages, and the adverse effects of pollution, they are starting to realize that it is not sufficient just to talk about military security, as in protecting the citizens of a country from a foreign threat, but it is also necessary to promote a concept of peace based upon ecological security, where humans are protected and nourished by natural processes (Mische, 1989).

Common to these peace educational endeavors is the desire to help people understand the roots of violence and to teach alternatives to violence. Although these types of peace education have different goals and problems of violence that they address, they share a concern about the devastation caused by violence and awareness about strategies to address that violence. Peace educators within these different contexts are teaching skills that can lead to successful management of conflict and attempting to build consensus about ways to stop the violence.

CONCLUSION

In spite of its tremendous growth in the twentieth century, peace education has not really taken hold in school systems around the world. A few countries have used United Nations' mandates to stimulate formal school-based peace education activities. Most countries have ignored them. Some countries like the Philippines and Uganda have mandated peace education in the public schools, but lack resources for training teachers in the various complexities of this new subject. In most countries, peace education is carried out informally in community settings and through national peace organizations, such as the large rallies held by Peace Now in Israel that attempt to garner citizen support for a less violent solution to the Palestinian-Israeli crisis than that being employed by the Israeli government. Local groups throughout the world, horrified by violence in their communities, attempt to convince their fellow citizens to oppose the violent policies of militaristic governments. This is by far the most widespread use of peace education at the beginning of the new millennium.

Formal school systems have largely ignored the educational insights provided by peace activist educators, mostly because of cultural and economic pressures to ramp up their curricula to include more math and science so that school graduates can compete in a high tech global economy. Peace education in most countries is seen as "soft" and not embraced by frightened citizens who fear imaginary or real enemies.

The threat of terrorism that grew from the end of the twenty century has made it hard for peace educators to convince school authorities to support efforts that contradict government "peace through strength" policies promoted to provide security for the citizens of that country. Furthermore, it is only recently that peace educators are starting to unify around a common curriculum for peace education that include its historic roots in international education as well as modern conventions for human rights, the feminist orientation on violence in interpersonal relations, a concern for the problems of structural violence, an emphasis upon building a culture of peace, and an urgency to address environmental issues—insights that were provided during the previous century rife with violent conflict (Harris & Morrison, 2003). Peace educators no longer solely concern themselves with interstate rivalry but also study ways to resolve intrastate violence and the chaos that comes from identity and religious-based conflicts. They have added to their tool boxes conflict resolution, forgiveness, and violence prevention skills, practical teachings that counterbalance the geopolitical approaches taken by political scientists concerned with wars between nations. The foundation for a new discipline has been built, leaving future peace educators to figure out how to erect a mighty peace palace.

REFERENCES

Addams, J. (1907). *Newer ideals of peace*. New York: MacMillan.

Banta, B. (1993). *Peaceful peoples: An annotated bibliography*. Metuchen, NJ: Scarecrow Press.

Bar-Tal, D. (2002). The elusive nature of peace education. In G. Salomon & B. Nevo (Eds.), *Peace education: The concepts, principles, and practices around the world* (pp. 27-36). Mahwah, NJ: Erlbaum.

Brocke-Utne, B. (1985). *Educating for peace: A feminist perspective*. New York: Pergamon Press.

Comenius, J. (1969). *A reformation of schools* (S. Harlif, Trans.). Menston (Yorks): Scholar Press. (Original work published 1642)

Eliot, T. S. (1936). *The hollow men. Collected poems of T.S. Eliot*. New York: Harcourt Brace.

Hamann B. (1996). *Bertha von Suttner*. Syracuse, NY: Syracuse University Press.

Harris, I. (1988). *Peace education*. Jefferson, NC: McFarland.

Harris, I., & M. Morrison. (2003). *Peace education* (2nd edition). Jefferson, NC: McFarland.

Mische, P. (1989). Ecological security and the need to reconceptualize sovereignty. *Alternatives, 14*(4), 389-428.

Montessori, M. (1974). *Education for a new world*. Thiruvanmiyur, India: Kalakshetra Press. (Original work published 1946)

Read, H. (1949). *Education for peace*. New York: C. Scribner's Sons.

Reardon, B. (1988). *Comprehensive peace education: Educating for global responsibility*. New York: Teachers College Press.

Salomon, G. (2002). The nature of peace education: Not all programs are created equal. In G. Salomon & B. Nevo (Eds.), *Peace education: The concepts, principles, and practices around the world* (pp. 3-14). Mahwah, NJ: Erlbaum.

Sandy, S. (2001). Conflict resolution in schools: "Getting there." *Conflict Resolution Quarterly, 19*(2), 237-250.

Scanlon, D. (1959). The pioneers of international education: 1817-1914. *Teacher's College Record, 4*, 210- 219.

Stomfay-Stitz, A. (1993). *Peace education in America 1828-1990, sourcebook for education and research*. Metuchen, NJ: Scarecrow Press.

CHAPTER 3

JOHN DEWEY AND PEACE EDUCATION

Charles F. Howlett

INTRODUCTION

John Dewey remains one of America's most preeminent philosophers and educational theorists. After World War I, he applied his instrumentalism and progressive education ideas to the advancement of world peace. Dewey's peace education was based on the view that teaching subjects like history and geography should be premised on the goal of promoting internationalism. His educational objective was to counter the philistine notion of patriotism and nationalism developed by individual nation-states which had been a basic cause of war.

BACKGROUND

Born in Vermont on October 20, 1859 and later educated at the University of Vermont (AB) and Johns Hopkins (PhD), John Dewey established himself as one of the leading philosophers in the field of pragmatism while teaching at the University of Chicago in the 1890s. The

Encyclopedia of Peace Education, pp. 25–31
Copyright © 2008 by Information Age Publishing
All rights of reproduction in any form reserved.

increasing dominance of evolutionary biology and psychology in his thinking led to the abandonment of the Hegelian theory of ideas and the acceptance of an instrumental theory of knowledge that conceived of ideas as tools or instruments in the solution of problems encountered in the environment. Prior to an appointment at Columbia University in 1904, Dewey's writings on schooling and education had already gained him a widespread audience. In *The School and Society* (1899) and *The Child and the Curriculum* (1902), he argued that the educational process must be built upon the interest of the child, that it must provide opportunity for the interplay of thinking and doing in the child's classroom experience, that schools should be organized as a miniature community, that the teacher should be a guide and coworker with pupils rather than a rigid taskmaster assigning a fixed set of lessons and recitations, and that the goal of education is the growth of the child. His crowning work, *Democracy and Education* (1916a), solidified his reputation in the history of American education.

But nothing prepared John Dewey for the events taking place in the world from 1914-1918. Despite being hailed as America's foremost educational philosopher, the Great War tested Dewey's mettle. During World War I, he reasoned that the use of force might provide a useful and efficient means for bringing about the goal of a democratically organized world order. Writing for his *International Journal of Ethics* and *New Republic* readers in "Force and Coercion" and "Force, Violence and Law," he commented that armed force was morally correct and war legally justified (Dewey, 1916b, 1916c).

What he did not count on was the stinging rebuke he received from his former Columbia student, Randolph Bourne. Bourne challenged Dewey's support for war by pointing out that the esteemed philosopher's instrumentalism had trapped him into miscalculating the relationship of the war to true national interests and democratic values. In a powerfully written article, "Twilight of Idols," Bourne (1917) argued that Dewey's excessive optimism caused him to overestimate the power of intelligence and underestimate the force of violence and irrationality.

CONTRIBUTIONS TO PEACE EDUCATION

It was Bourne's telling criticism that Dewey's support for war was technique conscious and morally blind that led to the Columbia philosopher's promotion of peace education after the war. In the postwar years, Dewey's interest in peace education was defined by a curious mixture of moralistic beliefs, democratic values, and nonreligious ethics. The basic thrust of his pragmatic philosophy and peace education efforts after 1918 was formulating the method of intelligence in such discriminating fashion as to minimize the appeal to nationalistic propaganda. Eliminating the institution of war required an educational program that would reconstruct existing social and political habits. The tragedies of the war convinced Dewey that schools could serve as a basis for dynamic change. Given proper direction, schools could become dynamic instead of reflexive agencies; as instruments of reform, schools could search out and reinforce concrete patterns to remake society in the name of peace while at the same time enabling each student to realize his or her potential for building a nonviolent world.

During the years between the two world wars, Dewey energetically examined ways in which peace education could become an effective instrument in promoting global understanding as opposed to the more traditional patriotic indoctrination that was currently doled out in schools and textbooks. Specifically, efforts for establishing world peace and universal citizenship were based upon a social science approach to education. Dewey insisted that there were two subjects that represented the foundation blocks necessary for building international understanding: geography and history. He believed that geography and history enabled students to reconstruct the past in order to cope with the present. Both subjects were necessary for overcoming some of the more sinister aspects of chauvinism which were being taught as citizenship in the schools.

When it came to the study of geography, for instance, Dewey applied his child-centered concepts and school as community into a more detailed investigation of peoples and their societies. Tying the notion of peace to global awareness required ways of teaching geography that would "help students gain insight into both nature and society, and which will help them apply what they learn … to their study of social and political problems" (Dewey, 1927, pp. 174-75). The proper teaching of geography to young students must take into account the study of all peoples, cultures, habits, occupations, art, and societies' contributions to the development of culture in general. For teachers, it was important that they stopped "worrying about the height of mountains and the length of rivers. When we do give consideration to these things, it must be in the context of cultural development" (Dewey, 1939, pp. 725-28).

Teaching geography to impressionable young minds had to become dynamic in order to act as a catalyst necessary for shaping a global picture. "Geography is a topic that originally appeals to imagination—even to the romantic imagination" Dewey (1916a, p. 212) asserted. "The variety of peoples and environment, their contrast with familiar scenes, furnishes infinite stimulation" (p. 212). As an important part of the curriculum, necessary for fostering global cooperation, "instruction in geography ... should be intellectually more honest, should bring students into gradual contact with the actual realities of contemporary life and not leave them to make acquaintance with these things in [a] surprised way" (Dewey, 1958, p. 4a).

The teaching of history should also promote the goal of peace by divorcing itself from the past emphasis on the study of dates, military heroes, and battles. What Dewey stressed in the curriculum was for teachers to focus more on the social meaning of history: "History is not the story of heroes, but an account of social development; it provides us with knowledge of the past which contributes to the solution of social problems of the present and the future" (quoted in Clopton & Tsuin-Chen, 1973, p. 277). Present-day problems, such as wars, should be examined in their historical setting in order "to determine the origin of the problem; examine past efforts to deal with the problem; find out what sort of situation caused it to become a problem" (quoted in Clopton & Tsuin-Chen, 1973, p. 277). Knowledge of the past, coupled with a forward-looking approach to problem solving and values clarification, characterized Dewey's conception of history as moral imperative. "Intellectual insight into present forms of associated life," Dewey (1916a) insisted,

> is necessary for a character whose morality is more than colorless innocence. Historical knowledge helps provide such insight. The assistance which may be given by history to a more intelligent sympathetic understanding of the social situations of the present in which individuals share is a permanent and constructive moral asset. (p. 217)

One of Dewey's major contributions to the importance of peace education was his argument that in order to achieve international harmony, important changes in domestic institutional thinking would have to occur first. In *Human Nature and Conduct* (1922), Dewey observed that "History does not prove the inevitability of war, but it does prove that customs and institutions which organize native powers into certain patterns in politics and economics will also generate the war-pattern" (p. 115). The key to conflict control was to deflate the emotions and values attached to nationalism and substitute in its place a world order based on international law and organization. "Questions of prestige and honor are now of inflammatory importance," he wrote in the aftermath of the Great War, "because of the legalizing of war and the absence of a court; they will remain the main reliance in the technique of enlisting support of a war waged for unavowed reasons until war is outlawed" (Dewey, 1923, p. 15).

In an effort to promote international understanding, Dewey called for a school program in the 1920s that would foster an appreciation for internationalism and challenge the glorification of militarism. Applying the social science approach of Professor James Harvey Robinson's "New History" to the curriculum, Dewey charged that current social studies texts used in American classrooms were not only diminishing possibilities for creating an atmosphere of international cordiality, but also increasing the chances for domestic intolerance. Issues such as the importance of the Outlawry of War Movement, a World Court, and American military interference in the Caribbean were not being addressed. To counter this trend, Dewey's peace education program encouraged the development of a curriculum exploring the theme of nationalism within an international context.

His peace curriculum was designed around promoting an attitude of world patriotism. "We need a curriculum in history, geography, and literature," he informed readers in one of his most important articles on the subject titled, "The Schools as a Means of Developing a Social Consciousness and Social Ideals in Children,"

> which will make it more difficult for the flames of hatred and suspicion to sweep over this country in the future, which indeed will make this impossible, because when children's minds are in the formative period, we shall have fixed in them through the medium of the schools, feelings of respect and friendliness for the other nations and peoples of the world. (Dewey, 1923, p. 516)

War as an institution thrives because no one is taught to question contemporary values and beliefs. The true value of his peace education program was in fostering new moral values in schoolchildren which would offset institutional habits. Challenging conservative critics who argued that war is part of human nature, Dewey responded by saying that

> War and the existing economic regime have not been discussed primarily on their own account. They are crucial cases of the relation existing between original impulse and acquired habit.... A truer psychology locates the difficulty elsewhere. It shows that the trouble lies in the inertness of established habit. (Dewey, 1922, p. 125)

The real key to Dewey's peace education program, however, and one that is relevant today, is transforming the notion of nationalism into a more transnational perspective. He was well aware of how successful nationalism was in the unification of Germany, and he attempted to use that historical experience in schools in order to develop "a new movement in education to preserve what was socially most useful in the national heritage and to meet the issue of the emerging international society" (quoted in Curti, 1967, p. 1109). The age-old identification of patriotism with "national interests," one fostered by habit and training, which inevitably led to exclusivity, suspicion, jealousy, and dislike for other national cultures had to be subordinated to broader conceptions of human welfare. The peace education program Dewey encouraged between the World Wars was one that

> binds people together in co-operative human pursuits and results, apart from geographical limitation. The secondary and provisional character of national sovereignty in respect to the fuller, freer, and more fruitful association and intercourse of all human beings with one another must be instilled as a working disposition of the mind. (quoted in Curti, 1967, p. 1109)

CONCLUSION

John Dewey's interest in peace education was inspired, in part, by the stinging condemnation he received for supporting President Woodrow Wilson's war aims in 1917. To his credit, he took those criticisms to heart and examined ways in which his social and political philosophy could further the interests of peace education in American schooling. Dewey proclaimed

> The lesson to be learned is that human attitudes and efforts are the strategic center for promotion of the generous aims of peace among nations; promotion of economic security; the use of political means in order to advance freedom and equality; and the world-wide cause of democratic institutions. (Dewey, 1946, p. 30)

Following this line of thought, he continued, "is bound to see that it carries with it the basic importance of education in creating the habits and the outlook that are able and eager to secure the ends of peace, democracy, and economic stability" (Dewey, 1946, p. 30). Even the horrors of World War II and the advent of the atomic bomb did not deter him from his goal of using schools to foster international understanding. He held onto that belief until his death in 1952.

Indeed, since the Vietnam War, there have been a number of peace education and peace studies programs created at colleges and universities throughout the United States. Many of these programs and peace courses have integrated Dewey's relativistic thought as an instrument for encouraging international understanding and domestic social justice. The real problem remains, however, at the elementary and secondary levels in American education. There, patriotic citizenship continues to be a powerful force in shaping young minds. It was in this area of learning that

Dewey directed most of his efforts during the interwar period. In calling for a peace education program in schooling, Dewey encouraged the creation of a curriculum emphasizing the development of an attitude which would accomplish the following: promoting the idea of world patriotism; using the social sciences, especially geography and history, as a bridge for understanding other cultures; and rectifying the more sinister aspects of patriotism and nationalism that have been a basic cause of war between nations. His peace education ideas also challenged the role of teachers and urged them to incorporate the values of peace and global cooperation among nations in their curricula. The promotion of the human community in education, Dewey (1971) maintained,

> is the responsibility of conserving, transmitting, rectifying and expanding the heritage of values we have received that those who come after us may receive it more solid and secure, more widely accessible and more generously shared than we have received it. (p. 87)

That article of faith was his educational blueprint and instrument for establishing a lasting peace.

REFERENCES

Bourne, R. (1917, October). Twilight of idols. *Seven Arts*, 688-702.

Clopton, R. W., & Ou, T.-C. (Eds.). (1973). *John Dewey: Lectures in China, 1919-1920.* Honolulu, HI: University of Hawaii Press.

Curti, M. (1967, Winter). John Dewey and nationalism. *Orbis, X,* 1109.

Dewey, J. (1899). *The school and society.* Chicago: University of Chicago Press.

Dewey, J. (1902). *The child and the curriculum.* Chicago: University of Chicago Press.

Dewey, J. (1916a). *Democracy and education.* New York: Macmillan.

Dewey, J. (1916b). Force and coercion. *International Journal of Ethics, 26,* 359-367.

Dewey, J. (1916c). Force, violence and the law. *New Republic, 5,* 295-297.

Dewey, J. (1922). *Human nature and conduct.* New York: Henry Holt.

Dewey, J. (1923). *Outlawry of war: What it is and is not.* Chicago: American Committee for the Outlawry of War

Dewey, J. (1927). *The public and its problems.* New York: Henry Holt.

Dewey, J. (1939). Education and American culture. In J. Ratner (Ed.), *Intelligence in the modern world* (pp. 725-728). New York: Random House.

Dewey, J. (1946). *The problems of men.* New York: Philosophical Library.

Dewey, J. (1958). *Experience and nature.* New York: Dove.

Dewey, J. (1971). *A common faith.* New Haven, CT: Yale University Press.

CHAPTER 4

MARIA MONTESSORI AND PEACE EDUCATION

Cheryl Duckworth

Averting war is the work of politicians; establishing peace is the work of educators.

—Maria Montessori

As the field of peace education develops, scholar-practitioners increasingly consider and debate who the founders of this field might be. For a field simultaneously as old as Confucius and as young as the United Nations, this is not a clear cut task. Major spiritual leaders such as Buddha, Muhammad, or Jesus Christ are sometimes considered "peace educators," as their lives and teachings are considered by millions to be examples of ethical and peaceable living. This speaks to the relevance of peace studies and peace education to many other disciplines; indeed peace and conflict resolution programs are inherently multidisciplinary, and draw on other fields such as sociology, history, anthropology, psychology, and literature to probe the origins of conflicts and what might practically be done about them. This nebulousness can trouble peace scholars and educators when trying to define the field and its foundational figures and theories.

Encyclopedia of Peace Education, pp. 33–37
Copyright © 2008 by Information Age Publishing
All rights of reproduction in any form reserved.

Before exploring a major figure in peace education, Dr. Maria Montessori, I should take a moment to define how I am using "peace education" in this context. It is quite a broad umbrella, and the phrase has been used to suggest anything from teaching peer mediation or conflict resolution skills to students, to curriculum about diversity, disarmament, or environmentalism or advocacy against poverty. Much of this complexity stems from the fact that methods and aspects of peace-building abound. This appropriately reflects the complexity of the causes of conflict. I am personally comfortable with this "big tent." Peace-building entails the active furthering of social and economic justice and peace education prepares students for this task.

Maria Montessori is most typically associated with child-led learning. By this, she believed that human beings are natural learners and that if students (often far younger than traditional methods dared) were immersed in environments rich with puzzles and problems to explore, they would learn instinctively similar to Vygotsky's theory (as cited in Van der Veer, 1994). In her model, the teacher facilitates the student's learning, but the student's passions and imagination are what lead, as she details in *Education and Peace* (1949). Similar to seminal American educator, John Dewey, her results were astounding: children thought to have significant mental challenges were successful learners (Lewis, n.d.). As most educators know, her methods gave birth to a movement in education that thrives globally today, with thousands of Montessori schools throughout North and South America, Europe, and Asia. She is, however, popularly known by some as a founder of peace education although this is not universally accepted.

Montessori's (1949) own writings explicitly make a connection to education for peace. She passionately argued (most notably before the United Nations) that education was a means—perhaps the only genuine means—of eliminating war once and for all. Without explicit and intentional moral and spiritual education, she believed, humankind would inevitably revert to its habit of war. Values such as global citizenship, personal responsibility, and respect for diversity, she argued, must be both an implicit and explicit part of every child's (and adult's) education. These values in Montessori education are every bit as crucial as the subjects of math, language or science. She wrote in *Education and Peace*,

> Peace is a goal that can only be attained through common accord, and the means to achieve this unity for peace are twofold: first, an immediate effort to resolve conflicts without recourse to violence—in other words, to prevent war—and second, a long-term effort to establish a lasting peace among men. (p. 27)

Teaching global citizenship is the explicit fostering of both a specific set of knowledge and a particular set of values in students (and teachers, for that matter). The specific curriculum might include addressing the causes of war and poverty, communication and other conflict resolution skills, disarmament or so on; the values would usually include and appreciation for diversity and nonviolence. Montessori's unique methods reinforce this commitment to fostering global citizens who would live out the values of and actively work for peace. This is for several pedagogical reasons. One, the fostering of independent critical thought (at age-appropriate levels, of course), as Montessori's contemporary John Dewey also emphasized, is vital to the survival of a democracy.

Citizens are less likely to be manipulated and mislead into a war not in their interests when they have developed a habit of informed reflection. Ironically, it was the infamous Nazi Goering who, while awaiting the Nuremberg trials in 1946, also expressed this point:

> Why, of course, the people don't want war. Why should some poor slob on a farm want to risk his life in a war when the best he can get out of it is to come back to his farm in one piece?... Voice or no voice, the people can always be brought to the bidding of the leaders. That is easy. All you have to do is tell them they are being attacked, and denounce the peacemakers for lack of patriotism and exposing the country to danger. It works the same in any country. (Goering, 1946)

Consciously developing the habit of critical and independent thought can protect men and women from such propaganda.

Second, as another significant figure in peace education, Elise Boulding (1979), often wrote that Montessori's methods explicitly fostered imagination by allowing the student to explore his interests and passions. What does this mean for a more peaceful world? I would argue that, just as the habit of independent and critical thought provides a manner of protection for democracy, prioritizing imagination in education can significantly contribute to solving the common problems we all face. Social entrepreneurs provide just one recent example. In the classroom, this might become student leadership in the community, as in some classrooms where students have undertaken environmental projects, taught other students or participated in local politics.

Yet the above features of imagination and a habit of critical, independent thought, while crucial to developing students who can contribute to building a more just and peaceful world, can be considered indirect connections between Montessori's methods and peace education. There are numerous explicit connections as well. Montessori deplored the lack of moral and social education that she observed in the typical public school. As Montessori (1949) wrote, "Any education that rejects and represses the promptings of the moral self is a crime" (p. xiv). Indeed, as states are the social institutions which commonly wage war, it is worth asking if currently public school systems are capable of authentic peace education. This question underscores Montessori's pedagogical revolution.

Of course, the methods of discipline or classroom management in Montessori education must reinforce what peace scholars refer to as "positive peace." Norwegian peace scholar Johan Galtung (1969) further developed this theory, defining positive peace as the presence such human values as justice, harmony, freedom, and equality. Negative peace—which is not at all a negative thing—is the absence of violence. As Montessori (1949) wrote, "The question of peace cannot be discussed properly from a merely negative point of view ... in the narrow sense of avoiding war.... Inherent in the very meaning of the word *peace* is the positive notion of constructive social reform" (p. xi). Thus, peace-building activities such as peace marches, community building forums such as interreligious dialogues, or advocacy against poverty developing such as the fair trade or debt cancellation movements, become an important feature of peace education. The Montessorian approach to peace can scarcely be called "passivism"; there is, in fact, nothing passive about it.

For peace education to be effective, the methods teachers and administrators use must be consistent with the values purportedly being taught to students. They must be modeled as well. The implicit curriculum must harmonize with the explicit curriculum. Montessori's methods reflect this as well. The emphasis is on self-discipline, rather than discipline imposed from outside. What might this look like in practical terms? Students would be involved in forming and enforcing the rules of their community, for one. Second, when undesired behavior does occur, the manner in which this is handled must honor the humanity of both the student who exhibited the behavior, as well as any victims.

As one may expect, this is the aspect of Montessori's methods most commonly critiqued as idealistic and naïve. Montessori and her followers may well make two replies to this. First, Montessori classrooms by their nature reduce undesirable behavior as students are genuinely engaged in their work. Second, one can observe from many public schools, given literacy and drop-out rates, that the "carrot and stick" approach is not working. If students are never given real choices as they grow, it is not realistic to expect them to suddenly acquire this skill upon graduation. Hence developing internal *self*-discipline is a vital outcome of Montessorian and other types of peace education.

Dr. Maria Montessori is a seminal figure in peace education. However, beyond merely producing theory, she developed concrete pedagogy for peace, one that is currently still thriving throughout the globe

(Duckworth, 2006). Her methodology focused on the development of the whole child and prized the creative and critical thinking skills, as well as relational skills, which are so critical in men and women who will be both inspired and equipped to build lasting peace.

REFERENCES

Boulding, E. (1979). *Children's rights and the wheel of life*. Edison, NJ: Transaction.

Duckworth, C. (2006). Teaching peace: A dialogue on the Montessori method. *Journal of Peace Education, 3*(1), 39-53.

Galtung, J. (1969). Violence, peace, and peace research. *Journal of Peace Research, 6*(3), 167-191.

Goering, H. (1946). *Urban legends quotes*. Retrieved November 12, 2007, from http://www.snopes.com/quotes/goering.asp

Lewis, C. (n.d.). As the sun shows itself at dawn. *Free Radical Online*. Retrieved November 12, 2007, from http://freeradical.co.nz/content/20/20lewis.php

Montessori, M. (1949). *Education and peace*. (H. R. Lane, Trans.). Chicago: Henry Regerny.

Van der Veer, R. (1994) *The Vygotsky reader*. Chapel Hill, NC: Blackwell.

CHAPTER 5

PAULO FREIRE AND PEACE EDUCATION

Lesley Bartlett

WHO WAS PAULO FRIERE?

Paulo Freire (1921-1997) was one of the best known and most influential radical education theorists in the twentieth century; his impact upon peace education, adult education, nonformal education, and critical literacy has been incalculable. Born in 1921 in Recife, in the Brazilian Northeast, Freire was raised in a middle-class family that hit hard times during the Great Depression. As a result, Freire directly experienced the impact of poverty on educational opportunities in a way that marked his entire career. Freire's participation in Recife's Movement for Popular Culture and his work for the University of Recife's Cultural Extension department greatly influenced his critique of educational inequalities and his remarkable approach to pedagogy.

Freire's early career was strongly influenced by the extraordinary political and cultural changes occurring in Latin America and the Caribbean. The Cuban Revolution (1959-1961) inspired socialist movements throughout the region; further, in the wake of the Second Vatican Council (1965), the Catholic Church increasingly embraced

Encyclopedia of Peace Education, pp. 39–45
Copyright © 2008 by Information Age Publishing
All rights of reproduction in any form reserved.

liberation theology and a commitment to the poor. Freire's formative period coincided with a general effervescence of radical politics in the Brazilian Northeast: peasant leagues demanded labor rights for rural workers; the Catholic Church formed "base communities" at the local level to involve lay people in interpretations of the Bible and the conduct of the Church's work; cultural circles focused on promoting popular culture and social critique formed throughout the region; and leftist leaders were elected at municipal, state, and federal levels. Because literacy was a requirement to vote at that time (and, indeed, until 1988 in Brazil), the Left focused energy on teaching literacy in order to build a populist political base.

In this context, Freire rose to prominence for his radical humanist pedagogy. In 1963, Freire was hired by the federal Ministry of Education to work for SUDENE (Superintendência de Desenvolvimento do Nordeste or Northeast Development Board) to develop educational projects. Upon invitation from local politicians, Freire and his colleagues conducted a "dialogical" literacy campaign in Angicos. Soon afterward, President João Goulart's populist national administration invited Freire to coordinate a national literacy campaign. This plan was aborted by the military coup in 1964. When the coup leaders exiled Freire, they ironically set up the conditions for his ideas to gain international attention. After a period in Chile and a shorter stint at Harvard University's School of Education, Freire joined the Department of Education at the World Council of Churches in Geneva. From that position, he actively participated in projects in Latin America and Africa.

When, after 15 years of exile, the military dictatorship began gradually to give way to re-democratization, Freire returned to his beloved Brazil. He joined the Workers Party, a new effort to invigorate and institutionalize the Left's involvement with formal politics. Freire wrote and taught actively during this period. With his characteristic determination to join theory and practice, Freire took on the daunting task of serving as Minister of Education for the city of São Paulo from 1988 to 1991. At the time of his death in 1997, Freire had authored or coauthored over a period of 30 years more than 20 books whose content significantly reshaped the way that educators think about the purpose and promise of schooling.

FREIRE'S KEY CONCEPTS

Freire's personal experiences deeply shaped his conceptual development. This chapter provides a necessarily partial overview of Freire's core tenets, including: education as a political act; banking versus problem-posing education; dialogue and critical consciousness; democratic teacher-student relationships; and the coconstruction of knowledge since they are foundational concepts that have been utilized in the field of peace education.

Education as a Political Act

Freire's major contribution to the field of peace education is the insight that education is, necessarily, a form of politics. He averred that schooling is never neutral; instead, it always serves some interests and impedes others. Freire's magnetism lies in his insistence that schooling can be used for liberation, just as it has been used for oppression. He argued that through liberatory education, people come to understand social systems of oppression and equip themselves to act to change those situations. Educators, then, must reconceptualize their labor as political work and "must ask themselves for whom and on whose behalf they are working" (Freire, 1985, p. 80).

In *Pedagogy of the Oppressed* (1970/1990), Freire introduced a radical distinction that has since become an enduring feature of progressive educational thought: the difference between what he called "banking" and "problem-posing" education. For Freire,

> [Banking education] attempts, by mythicizing reality, to conceal certain facts which explain the way men exist in the world.... Banking education resists dialogue; problem-posing education regards dialogue as indispensable to the act of cognition which unveils reality. Banking education treats students as objects of assistance; problem-posing education makes them critical thinkers.... Problem-posing education bases itself on creativity and stimulates true reflection and action upon reality, thereby responding to the vocation of men as beings who are authentic only when engaged in inquiry and creative transformation. (p. 71)

Banking education is a relationship of domination in which the teacher has knowledge that she deposits in the heads of the passive objects of assistance—her students. Banking education maintains students' immersion in a culture of silence and positions them as objects, outside of history and agency.

In contrast to banking education, Freire proposes a problem-posing education. Problem-posing education encourages students to become active in thinking about and acting upon their world. Problem-posing education relies upon dialogue and critical consciousness, democratic teacher-student relationships, the cocreation of knowledge through interaction, and a curriculum grounded in students' interests and experiences.

Dialogue and Critical Consciousness

For Freire (1970/1990), dialogue was a key component of problem-posing education. Dialogue, he wrote, is "the encounter between men [sic], mediated by the world, in order to name [that is, to change] the world" (p. 76). In *Pedagogy of the Oppressed*, Freire insisted that dialogical encounters help students to develop critical consciousness of social, political, and economic contradictions so that they can take action against them (p. 43). Coming to critical consciousness requires analyzing, interactively and through dialogue, who is and is not allowed access to resources and opportunities, and how access is allowed or denied. Critical consciousness ultimately requires questioning the status quo rather than taking it as given. Though Freire's early work suggested that critical consciousness would somehow necessarily lead to social action, his later work amended that claim. Nonetheless, the goal of problem-posing education is praxis, which is "reflection and action upon the world in order to transform it" (p. 33).

Democratic Teacher-Student Relationships

According to Freire (1970/1990), problem-posing education can only occur within egalitarian, respectful relations:

> dialogue cannot occur between those who want to name the world and those who do not wish this naming—between those who deny other men the right to speak their word and those whose right to speak has been denied to them. Those who have been denied their primordial right to speak their word must first reclaim and prevent the continuation of this dehumanizing aggression. (pp. 76-77)

Problem-posing education relies on a revolutionary, respectful relationship between teacher and student. Democratic educators seek to replace the traditional teacher-student hierarchy with egalitarian interactions. In *Pedagogy of the Oppressed*, Freire (1970/1990) wrote that problem-posing education "cannot exist, however, in the absence of a profound love for the world and its people.... Founding itself upon love, humility, and faith, dialogue becomes a horizontal relationship of which mutual trust between the dialoguers is a logical consequence" (pp. 77-78).

Further, Freire (1970/1990) suggested that problem-posing education revolutionizes the teacher-student relationship:

> through dialogue, the teacher of the students and the students of the teacher cease to exist and a new term emerges: teacher-student with students-teachers.... [T]he teacher is no longer merely the one who teachers, but one who is himself taught in dialogue with the students, who in their turn while being taught also teach. (p. 67)

Freire's (1994) early call for a "horizontal" relationship generated a staggering amount of debate over the teacher's role in a democratic classroom. In his later writings, Freire refined his notion of directivity and the teacher-student relationship. In *Pedagogy of Hope*, he explained: "Dialogue between teachers and students does not place them on the same footing professionally; but it does mark the democratic position between them" (pp. 116-117). In his "talking" books of the 1980s and 90s, Freire (1985) distinguished between authoritative and authoritarian teachers:

> I have never said that the educator is the same as the pupil. Quite the contrary, I have always said that whoever says that they are equal is being demagogic and false. The educator is different from the pupil. But this difference, from the point of view of the revolution, must not be antagonistic. The difference becomes antagonistic when the authority of the educator, different from the freedom of the pupil, is transformed into authoritarianism. This is the demand I make of the revolutionary educator. For me, it is absolutely contradictory when the educator, in the name of the revolution, takes power over the method and orders the pupil, in an authoritarian way, using this difference that exists. This is my position, and therefore it makes me surprised when it is said that I defend a nondirective position. How could I defend the fact that the nature of the educational process is always directive whether the education is given by the bourgeoisie or the working class. (p. 76)

The Coconstruction of Knowledge

According to Freire (1970/1990), new knowledge is produced in the classroom from the interaction between students' and teachers' knowledges. "Knowledge," according to Freire, "emerges only through invention and re-invention, through the restless, impatient, continuing, hopefully inquiry men [sic] pursue in the world, with the world, and with each other" (p. 58).

Freire (1970/1990) consistently advocated pedagogies, curricula, and learning based in the students' "reality." In *Pedagogy of the Oppressed*, he asserted, "The starting point for organizing the program content of education or political action must be the present, existential, concrete situation, reflecting the aspirations of the people" (p. 85). This idea has become a core principle of critical pedagogy, peace education, and, in many ways, of progressive education more generally: education should be relevant, and it should be grounded in the experiences and interests of students.

Fundamentally, Freire advocated that teachers should *respect* students' knowledge, *begin with* student's knowledge, and remain *humble* about the limitations of their own knowledge. He warned about the dual threat of elitism, or the rejection of popular knowledge as backward or simplistic, and basicism, or the "exaltation or mystification" of popular knowledge (Schugurensky, 1998, p. 24).

In *Pedagogy of Hope* (1994), Freire stated that he did not wish to suggest that popular knowledge was somehow, by itself, sufficient: "it is unacceptable to advocate an educational practice that is satisfied with rotating on the axis of 'common sense'" he wrote (p. 58). Responding to charges that his focus on popular knowledge would limit students' understanding of global structures, he asserted, "never ... have I said that these programs ... ought to remain absolutely bound up with local reality" (p. 86). Instead, education should start with but go beyond student's local knowledge:

> The educator needs to know that his or her "here" and "now" are nearly always the educands' "there" and "then." Even though the educator's dream is not only to render his or her "here-and-now" with them, or to understand and rejoice that educands have gotten beyond their "here" so that this dream is realized, she or he must begin with the educands' "here" and not with her or his own. At the very least, the educator must keep account of the existence of his or her educands' "here" and respect it. Let me put it this way: you never get there by starting from there, you get there by starting from some here. This means, ultimately, that the educator must not be ignorant of, underestimate, or reject any of the 'knowledge of living experience' with which educands come to school. (p. 58)

Later in the book, he added:

> we must not by-pass—spurning it as "good for nothing"—that which educands ... bring with them in the way of an understanding of the world.... With progressive education, respect for the knowledge of living experience is inserted into the larger horizon against which it is generated—the horizon of cultural context, which cannot be understood apart from its class particularities. (p. 85)

Freire (1998) recommended that all learning *begin* from students' experiential knowledge, and that it proceed by working with students to understand the "logic of these kinds of knowledge in relation to their contents" (p. 36).

Freire's philosophy thoroughly informs peace education pedagogy and practice. His complicated concept of conscientization provides the foundation of peace education's hope for a link between education and social transformation. His insistence on dialogue and his discussions of egalitarian teacher-student relations provide the basis for peace education pedagogy. Despite his death a decade ago, Freire's ideas continue to resound throughout the field.

REFERENCES

Freire, P. (1985). *The politics of education: Culture, power, and liberation* (D. Macedo, Trans.). South Hadley, MA: Bergin & Garvey.

Freire, P. (1990). *Pedagogy of the oppressed.* New York: Continuum Press. (Original work published 1970)

Freire, P. (1994). *Pedagogy of hope: Reliving pedagogy of the oppressed.* New York: Continuum.

Freire, P. (1998). *Pedagogy of freedom: Ethics, democracy, and civic courage.* Lanham, PA: Rowman & Littlefield.

Schugurensky, D. (1998). The legacy of Paulo Freire: A critical review of his contributions. *Convergence, 31*(1/2), 17-29.

SECTION II

Foundational Perspectives in Peace Education

The previous section examined the history of and influences on peace education while this section focuses squarely on the field to understand some of the perspectives that have shaped its emergence. These chapters examine the interplay of local realities and global issues and structures. The United Nations, though established as a meeting place for nation-states, is increasingly a forum for global civil society to interact and forge consensus on issues of peace and human rights. This section explores the perspectives of scholars shaping the form, content, ethical orientations, and organizational structure of research in the field as well as the institutions that have provided the contours of peace education practice.

QUESTIONS TO CONSIDER

- What are the core principles that guide peace education? How do the *form* and *content* of education interact to reflect these principles?

Encyclopedia of Peace Education, pp. 47–48
Copyright © 2008 by Information Age Publishing

- How do the micro- and macrolevels intersect and influence each other? In considering the sociological distinction between structure (macrolevel) and agency (microlevel), how can social change towards greater peace occur at the local, national, and international levels?
- The terms "structural" and "direct" violence indicate different types of limitations on human freedom. Consider examples of these forms of violence and how peace education—in formal and informal settings—might address these issues.

CHAPTER 6

FORM AND CONTENT OF PEACE EDUCATION

Johan Galtung

INTRODUCTION

When the peace research movement started at the end of the 1950s, the universities did not, in general, welcome it. Rather, the idea was picked up by research institutes, often with no attachment to teaching institutions at all. Today, we still bear the consequences of this: a movement strong on research and action, but weak on education, generally failing to bring findings into schools and universities. In short, despite the many professions to the contrary, peace education has probably not developed as significantly during the last decades, particularly in contrast to the considerable advances made in the fields of peace research and peace action.

One reason for this is the stranglehold of established educational institutions in most countries that affects all levels of education. What is taught usually reflects the past, which is simply handed over to the present so as to secure continuity into the future in conformity with national ideology and upper class thinking. Sincere peace research or peace action will often contrast with this type of perspective. One might

Encyclopedia of Peace Education, pp. 49–58
Copyright © 2008 by Information Age Publishing
All rights of reproduction in any form reserved.

assume that this would encourage more peace research groups and action groups to add peace education programs to their activities, but in general this has not happened, largely due to lack of funds, understaffing and overconcern with research and action. Peace education in schools and for the general public lags behind.

It is high time for this sad tradition to be broken and for peace education to be taken seriously. This would be one part of a larger transformation in which peace research, peace action, and peace education would become integrated into a natural whole. Keeping them apart is more a reflection of division of labor tendencies in surrounding societies than of any real necessity. In fact, the three fields could hardly be more intimately related.[1]

For example, a very important thread in peace research is historical: understanding how slavery was abolished, how socialist policies improved the material conditions of the masses, how anticolonization movements came into being and ultimately were somewhat successful, how emancipist and feminist movements improved the lot of women, and how mobilization against structural violence in general is possible.[2] These are all obvious themes for peace education as well.

There could also be research programs within peace education—not only research on images of peace, but on how and why they change, with or without peace action. Particularly significant would be research on unconventional communication, on new forms of peace education that are not only communicative but also can be seen as pure education at a high level that can function as vehicles of social change.

There are other linkages, as well. Both peace research and peace education will ultimately lead to peace action, if they are of any value, and any peace action will have its research and educational spin-offs and benefits. Nonetheless, because of how we divide labor, outside institutions should play a stronger role in shaping the need for peace education, and ultimately also the content, particularly if peace researchers and activists are caught unaware.

All over the world today there is talk about peace research and education. Examples of this trend are that (1) Peace education chairs are appearing in several universities; (2) There is a *demand* for peace curricula at all levels of education; but those who demand have only vague notions of what they ask for, and that is not necessarily their fault (Galtung, 1972). It is our fault as peace educators and researchers that we have not been able to present a sufficiently rich *supply* of information and materials to participate actively in this process. But it is not too late; we are still only at the beginning. It is in order to stimulate active participation in this process that this chapter has been written.

THE FORM OF PEACE EDUCATION

It may seem strange to start with the *form* rather than with the *content*, but there is a simple reason: the form may open some new possibilities that should also be reflected in the content. I hope to show here that there is a wide range of opportunities available to all who want to enter the field of peace education in one way or another. Although there is always room for expansion, we do not actually make effective use of all of the available options: lectures at universities, pamphlets and books, seminars and conferences, newspaper articles and magazine essays are just some of the possible vehicles of communication.[3]

First, the form of peace education has to be compatible with the idea of peace, that is, it has to exclude not only direct violence, but also structural violence. This is important because schools and universities are still important means of education and in the structure is the message.

Only rarely is education nowadays packaged with direct violence; the days of colonialism and corporal punishment are more or less gone. But structural violence remains and takes the usual forms: a highly vertical division of labor manifesting itself in one-way communication; the fragmentation of those on the receiving end preventing them from developing horizontal interaction that will allow them to organize and eventually turn the communication flow the other way; and the absence of true multilateralism in the education endeavor. All of this relates only to form, and if the content of education is also included, the structural violence of education becomes even more apparent.

Fundamentally, peace education should attempt to do away with this type of inherent violence. Any educational form should be evaluated in terms of its structure and the following questions should always be asked: Does it permit feedback? Does it bring people together in a joint endeavor rather than keeping them apart? Does it permit general participation, and is the total form of education capable of self-generated change? In short, is there dialogue that engages learners, rather than simply a message conveyed in educational settings?

A second basic problem has to do with the relationship between peace education and the traditional structure of formal schooling that is divided into primary, secondary, and tertiary levels. The question is usually asked: Why not incorporate peace education into the curricula at all three levels? Yet the answer may not be so obvious. It may in fact be true that at all three levels, the form of schooling itself would effectively counteract the very idea of peace education, and hence be harmful. It is naïve to believe that the content of a message will survive regardless of the form in which it is presented; in fact, the form may turn out to be even more important than the content.

Many students, at all educational levels, share the experience that their leisure reading provokes deeper insights and is more interesting and gratifying than their required reading for school. For many, the moment something is added to the curriculum, it accumulates dust and becomes gray and flat like everything else.

Additionally, in many countries the school system is centralized under one Ministry of Education with almost dictatorial powers over the curricula, controlled by bureaucrats or committees unable to reflect new ideas or quickly incorporate the demands of younger generations. The average age for the committee members is often very high, and the capacity for self-generated change after their own studies is so low that committees, at their best, reflect the dominant thinking of when they were young and, at worst, the dominant thinking of when their teachers or professors were young. In a quickly changing society—and particularly in a society where conceptions of development, conflict, and peace are changing so quickly—this is unacceptable. Something innovative may be squeezed through such machinery, but at the risk of becoming so flattened out that, even if the form of education was untouched, there would be little of the original content left.

Furthermore, even in countries that are highly decentralized, there will always be one state, province, district, city, or municipality more advanced than the others, more ready to experiment with new things than other, and more conservative locales. However, even if innovations are implemented only in one school or class, they can be valuable on a wider scale because of the demonstration effect.

Yet another difficulty is the strong tie between traditional schooling institutions and the social practice of sorting people into categories, and even classes, with the examination as the physical manifestation of this link. Using education as a sorting device is problematic for peace educators, since the idea of peace itself is antithetical to vertical social relations and hierarchies in any form. Hence, peace education should be seen as a way of achieving, individually and collectively, a higher level of consciousness, an awareness of social reality and solidarity in a joint learning community, not as a mechanism social classification. There should be no examinations of any kind in connection with peace education, no basis for an emerging class of peace specialists. Such devices may have a place in military academies and business schools, but not in institutions promoting peace insights.[4]

THE CONTENT OF PEACE EDUCATION

With an arsenal of possible forms at one's disposal, what can be communicated through peace education? In fact, it is only by keeping peace research, peace education, and peace action together that a strong formula for content can be developed.

One way of approaching content derives from the five phases of a peace research project. Of course, there are divided opinions on these phases. The five phases are as follows:

1. Analysis
2. Goal-formulation
3. Critique
4. Proposal-making
5. Action (Galtung, 1972)

Analysis of our present, real world describes basic facts to the extent that they are relevant to peace problems and at the same time pointing to major trends. The analysis would be dynamic in the sense of presenting a time perspective and static in the sense of giving an image of such major factors as the war system and the preparation for war. It also relates to problems of equity and freedom, which are both antonyms of dominance, but for different arenas and from different ideological traditions. Thus, this is the place to present and theoretically explain relevant facts, keeping in mind that there is always more than one theory that can be applied to the same set of data.

If this were all, peace studies would not differ from any other social science found today, and peace education would mirror education in, say, physics or geography. Hence, it is the subsequent four points that add the special flavor to both of these fields.

Goal formulation is an indispensable part of peace education. There has to be something concrete and explicit in the idea of peace: the world we would like to see. It is not enough to say that peace is the absence of something or the other; much more concrete images must be provided. Peace research, being born inside the traditional empiricist tradition, whether of the conservative or progressive varieties, has largely failed on this point. Rather, analysis has prevailed at the expense of goal-formulation, the latter being rejected rather summarily as "utopianism." And yet it is exactly these kinds of images that, throughout history, have driven people into great action, including the types of movements mentioned in the introduction.[5]

As a part of this aspect of peace research and peace education comes the general question of whether the goal is just any type of utopia, or is it a viable utopia? For instance, is it possible to have the absence of direct violence, equity in social interaction, and freedom for a considerable degree of human self-expression or self-realization? Or is it true, as some might assert, that of these three values, we can only have two and we shall have to choose which two, or even, as the pessimists might assert, one or even none at all? This type of discussion is rarely found in any educational curriculum at any level, probably causing a tremendous crippling of individual and collective human imagination in search for a better future combining that which cannot be combined.

Third, the critique. For any type of critique to be of interest, both data and values have to be present, which are made available in the first and second phases, respectively. The values become like a net thrown over our world, leading to very concrete conclusions in terms of highly value-oriented language, and where nobody can turn away from terms like "good" and "bad," or even language considerably more explicit than that.

This third phase goes beyond analysis to diagnosis, based on the more static aspects of empirical analysis, and prognosis based on the more dynamic aspects. An effort should be made to call the same dimensions by the same name, whether they refer to past, present, or future. After these phases, we will end up with critical images of these three different worlds, including dimensions that can be used to define both the preferred world and the real world.[6] That makes it possible to accommodate the real world, using data; the preferred world, the utopia, using values; and possibly also even more highly criticized world, a dystopia. To understand better the struggle of moving from the real world towards utopia, we need to understand what prevents the real world from becoming worse and even sliding into dystopia.

Fourth, proposal-making deals with how to get from the real world to the preferred world. Finding a transition path is a question of proposals about what to do, who should do it, when and where, how, and why it should be done. Proposal-making should be seen as a basic part of any peace education program. Indeed, no part would be more ideal for general participation than this. Any successful peace education program would make the participants really feel the tension between the preferred and the real worlds, and the danger looming from the rejected world would make participants feel it so intensely that proposal making becomes a necessity.[7]

This then leads into the fifth phase: peace action. One cannot suddenly truncate a process because it can no longer be contained within articles and books, paper and pencil exercises, or even discussion, but it becomes driven by necessity into something much more concrete: action.

This does not necessarily imply that each and every peace education program should include an action component such as a demonstration, a peacekeeping activity, or a peace building component.[8] We would, however, advocate discussions of concrete action, like a search for new forms of peace education or participation in a practice-oriented organization. In any other educational program, a nonverbal component is usually taken for granted: the laboratory exercises in chemistry, physics, and biology; the visit to civic and social institutions as a part of sociology, and so on. It can be so in peace education as well.[9]

There are problems connected with peace action, but with time, we are gaining much more experience with this aspect of education. Also, this is the point where peace education, peace action, and peace research really come together. For instance, students at a particular school might decide to recognize an emerging nation before their own government does. If thousands of schools did the same, according to clear peace criteria, this could even become an important form of nongovernmental foreign policy, and hence, have a widespread democratizing effect.[10]

In concrete school situations, as already mentioned, there are many examples of structural violence, and hence, many areas in which problems of peace can be actualized, such as bullying. It is naïve to think that peace education can be contained within the school systems of most countries without having some repercussions on the political system.[11] Traditional teaching of peace studies has been that of peaceful men—Lord Buddha, Jesus Christ, St. Francis of Assisi, Mahatma Gandhi, Albert Schweitzer, Martin Luther King Jr. being some of the prime examples—often with a heavy emphasis on their beliefs and attitudes rather than their action and behavior. This approach tends to focus on actors rather than structures, and is unacceptable from the point of view of peace studies, which would argue for including both.

Any analysis of structures would lead to pupils and students to use this analytical machinery on the school situation as well. In so doing, they would start asking questions about the division of labor (why are we treated as raw material to be processed through the school machinery?), about participation (why do we not participate more in the decisions regarding how schools are run and curricula developed?), and so on. In other words, students may not only have demands concerning the content of school curricula (why do we not learn about our country's military-industrial complex? about the weapons export of our country? about the true relations between rich and poor countries?), but also about the school structure itself. A higher level of consciousness among students can have the same effect at the secondary level of education as it has already had at the tertiary level in terms of action, including strikes and boycotts to back up demands.

CONCLUSION

Four related and central topics often arise in courses, seminars, and discussions on peace and a brief explanation is provided for each of these:

> *Development:* gives the opportunity to present basic values, trends, the state of affairs in the world in general and turn the discussion of peace towards positive peace, equity, and harmony;[12]
> *Conflict:* gives the opportunity to discuss what happens when goals, values, and interests are in conflict and discuss conflict creation, conflict dynamics, and conflict transformation and resolution;
> *Peace:* gives the opportunity to discuss how development and a creative approach to conflict can come together in the fight against direct as well as structural violence; and
> *Future:* gives the opportunity to project all of this onto the screen of the future, analyzing trends, and making proposals for action.

Everyone, however, must develop his/her own unique format and formula; there is no standard to be adhered to, as that would be contrary to the whole idea of autonomy in peace education.[13]

Finally, one note about the role of peace education: it should not overshadow peace action. One may object that peace education is needed for peace action, but the relation is not that simple. Peace education will work on the mind, although it may also imply some training. It is a fundamental bias of intellectuals, however, to believe that we human beings think first and then unleash our well-considered action. Very often we act first and if it works, we may develop a theory about it; if it does not work, some rationalization will take place.

That does not mean that a much higher level of peace consciousness may not change this state of affairs. The fact is that we do not even know what that would mean, what kind of world that would be. But it would certainly be a world where people would be less easily manipulated, and it is in pursuit of that kind of world that peace education would be a contribution.

ACKNOWLEDGMENT

This chapter is a highly reedited version of Galtung, J. (1975). *Peace: Research, education, action. Essays in peace research* (Vol. 1, pp. 317-333). Copenhagen, Denmark: Christian Ejlers. (Original work published 1968)

NOTES

1. For a theory of this approach, see Galtung (1977).
2. For a discussion of these societies, see Galtung (1970a).
3. An excellent proposal in this field has been made by Vithal Rajan (1972).
4. The most promising approach here seems to be the International Games, in the tradition started by Harold Guetzkow.
5. However, a basic finding of the book titled *Images of the World in the Year 2000*, published in 1976, coordinated by the European Social Science Center in Vienna, is exactly the very low level of future-oriented thinking, especially in the field of political affairs, according to the results of 9,000 interviews in 10 countries, 8 of them in Europe, with 200 questions.
6. This is the basic idea of the social indicator movement: to present values as dimensions that also can be used for ordinary descriptive analysis.
7. The idea was very simple: to ask all participants as a conclusion of four weeks with discussions of peace theory and peace practice to come up with some image of their ideal world and the steps needed to attain it. Since most people are asked to present their image of the present world and how to criticize and analyze it, it is not strange that there is an untapped reservoir in the direction indicated.
8. For a concrete proposal combining the elements treated under this heading, see Galtung (1970b).
9. See Galtung (1972).
10. See initiative headed by Professor Ivan Supek, which had a council of representatives from several universities.
11. In Norway, for instance, an oath of loyalty to the King is required of university professors.
12. It might perhaps be pointed out that conceptions of development, perhaps also conflict, seem to be changing much more quickly than conceptions of peace, which still to many seem to be related to balance of power and disarmament ideas, without going much deeper into the origins of peacelessness.
13. For an elaboration of this proposal, see Galtung (1968).

REFERENCES

Galtung, J. (1968). Training of peace specialists: A proposal. *International Peace Research Newsletter, 2,* 42-46.

Galtung, J. (1970a). Pluralism and the future of human society. Challenges for the future: *Proceedings from the Second International Futures Research Conference, Norway,* 271-308.

Galtung, J. (1970b). Towards a World Peace Academy: A proposal. *Essays in Peace Research, 1*(14), 291.

Galtung, J (1972, September). *Empiricism, criticism, constructivism: Three approaches to scientific activity.* Paper presented at the Third World Future Research Conference, Bucharest, Romania.

Galtung, J. (1977). Chemical structure and social structure: An essay on structuralism. In J. Galtung, M. Bunge, & M. Malitza (Eds.), *Mathematical approaches to international relations* (pp. 389-417). Bucharest, Romania: Romanian Academy of Social and Political Sciences.

Rajan, V. (1972). War and peace: Adult education in peace education. *Millennium Journal of International Studies, 1*(3), 50-66.

CHAPTER 7

CONCEPTUAL PERSPECTIVES IN PEACE EDUCATION

Magnus Haavelsrud

INTRODUCTION

A great variety of theories, definitions and practices are referred to in peace education. Since both "peace" and "education" are abstractions without any concrete and absolute meaning, it is not surprising that it is rather difficult to find widespread agreement about what peace education actually is.

This essay will discuss some important dimensions within which it is believed the major conceptual disagreements are to be found. This will be done in reference to three major components of the educational problematic: the content, method of communication, and organizational structure of the educational program. The choices made about these three components prove to be decisive in defining the substance of any educational program, including education for peace.

Some peace educators seem to judge only one or two of these three components as important. Thus, it is not difficult to find peace education projects that are limited to changing the content of education without questioning existing pedagogic methods or the organization of activities.

Encyclopedia of Peace Education, pp. 59–66

Some peace educators argue that only the form of learning-teaching interactions must be changed in order for the ideals of peace education to be realized. Still others are more system-oriented in their proposals, suggesting changes in the organizational structure in order to regulate educational interactions. It is contended, therefore, that disagreements about the substance of peace education are related to the importance given to each of the three components and also to the implicit or explicit choices that are made within each component.

CONTENT

So, what content is to be learned in peace education? No *absolute* answer is to be found in the literature about peace education or anywhere else on this topic. In the initial phase of developing its peace education program, UNESCO (United Nations Educational, Scientific, and Cultural Organization) (1974) proposed using a macro approach and selecting "the most important problems of mankind" (p. 3):

(a) the equality of rights of peoples, and the right of peoples to self-determination;

(b) the maintenance of peace; different types of war and their causes and effects; disarmament; the inadmissibility of using science and technology for warlike purposes and their use for the purposes of peace and progress; the nature and effect of economic, cultural and political relations between countries and the importance of international law for these relations, particularly for the maintenance of peace;

(c) action to ensure the exercise and observance of human rights, including those of refugees; racialism and its eradication; the fight against discrimination in its various forms;

(d) economic growth and social development and their relation to social justice; colonialism and decolonization; ways and means of assisting developing countries; the struggle against illiteracy; the campaign against disease and famine; the fight for a better quality of life and the highest attainable standard of health; population growth and related questions;

(e) the use, management and conservation of natural resources, pollution of the environment;

(f) preservation of the cultural heritage of mankind; and

(g) the role and methods of action of the United Nations system in effort to solve such problems and possibilities for strengthening and furthering its action. (pp. 3-4)

This proposal for peace education content is globally oriented, and the major problems of humankind are explicitly macro. How specific circumstances appear at various levels on the micro-macro spectrum is a most difficult and interesting problem involving questions of cause and effect between the levels. What, for instance, are the effects of enemy images propagated by governments for legitimating a war in shaping our consciousness? Or, in another example, what was the impact of the microlevel mobilization of peace demonstrators against the war in Iraq on February 15, 2003? This protest evolved into a macro force in terms of sheer numbers of people mobilized around the world, in spite of being hidden in the micro realities of, for example, the 2 million inhabitants of London and neighboring towns that gathered in Hyde Park. The hidden force of the morning had manifested itself by the evening, turning micro-level phenomena into a global movement. It was not strong enough to stop the war at that time, but these events add to others in a continuous flow of resistance against certain kinds of international behaviors.

It is evident that proposals for peace education content vary in relation to the macro-micro dimension. For instance, some peace educators define the content in terms of international and global problems whereas others define the content in relation to the everyday life and the context of the individual. In both cases, the initial disintegration of micro and macro may be temporary or permanent. If it is permanent, the segregation has an epistemological status, and if it is temporary, it may be grounded in a methodological belief that a complex problem needs to be simplified at the beginning of the educational experience. Thus, the goal may or may not be to understand the micro context in light of the macro context and vice versa, depending upon the duration of the strong segregation of micro-macro phenomena. In all cases, the strength and degree of permanence of any classification of this sort would carry with it a message of power on behalf of those who have made the decision to keep the categories apart.

Such integration or nonintegration of "here and now" with "there and then" is a major choice to make concerning the content. Further, it is important if one chooses to depart from the "here and now" context or the "there and then" context because this choice may influence the understanding of the totality, especially in regard to the question of causal relationships between micro and macro phenomena. Starting with "here and now," situations may give the impression that these are important in the explanation of the global totality, whereas starting with "there are then" may imply more emphasis upon seeing the global reality as a cause of micro phenomena.

The Spatial Dimension

The bridge built between the extreme micro level (the individual) and the extreme macro level (the world), may utilize various support points. Thus, relevant content in a peace education project may involve actors/parties at "in-between" levels such as the family, peer groups, neighbors, social class, ethnic, gender or age groups, town or local community, political parties, region, nation, or region of the world. The bridges may be built as two-way channels in which the situations at both ends are seen to be interrelated, or they may be one-way bridges that hinder the understanding of two-way causality.

Poverty is seen as a major problem to be solved. If the content is limited to the macro level, the problem of poverty may become a study of global statistics and trends. The problem of poverty may then become a global phenomenon without reference to the reality of the learner. A macro analysis will yield macro solutions to the problem. If, on the other hand, the problem of poverty is also seen in the specific contexts of the learners, they will be able to analyze the problem in light of the realities in their own contexts and also be able to suggest actions in that context to help solve the problem. The inclusion or exclusion of such cause-effect relationships between the micro and the macro levels is decisive for the content of peace education.

The Temporal Dimension

Apart from the problem of inclusion or exclusion on the spatial dimension, there is the problem of inclusion or exclusion of the temporal dimension. Reflection about an issue and its solution involves understanding the problem at various points in its development. The dispersion of the content of peace education over the following categories is therefore an important choice to make:

1. Historic knowledge: what was;
2. Diagnostic knowledge: what is;
3. Predictive knowledge: what will be;
4. Prescriptive knowledge: what ought to be; and
5. Knowledge about tactics and strategy: what can be done to change the situation from what it is to what it ought to be.

Action

So far, I have only discussed peace education in terms of reflection. A major choice to make concerning the content of peace education is whether it should include or exclude action for the solution of the problem. If action is included, the timing of it in relation to the reflection process is also important, that is, is it possible to develop a reflection process about a problem on the basis of some action already undertaken, or is action as part of the peace education content seen as desirable only as a result of a reflection and study process?

FORM

In some peace education projects, more emphasis is placed on teaching methods and learning than on the content as such. This is often grounded upon the principle that the educational interaction should be in harmony with the idea of peace. This could mean that teacher and students should be equal partners in the educational process. The teacher would be in dialogue with the students about a problem that interests both parties. The teacher does not necessarily have to be an expert who knows all about the problem. It should be apparent that any human, including a teacher, cannot be expected to possess all knowledge about the solution of societal problems. Only historic and diagnostic knowledge can be reproduced. Knowledge in the other categories has to be produced by all the participants in the educational situation. This reproduction and production of knowledge cannot be done only by the teacher if propaganda for and/or indoctrination of specific views are to be avoided.

This means that some knowledge about solving a social, political, economic or cultural problem can only be given through the active participation of those who are suffering the consequences of the problem and whose interest in solving the problem is not purely academic, but also emotional and practical. Thus, problem solving in this sense involves knowledge already produced in science about objective realities as well as knowledge to be produced in the educational setting. It is to be expected that the latter most often would apply to knowledge about the future (what will be, what ought to be) as well as to tactical and strategic knowledge. These three, as well as the realization of the action, may be seen as more dependent upon subjective viewpoints than upon "academic" knowledge about historical and present circumstances. Peace education forms are in contradiction to anti-dialogical methods, resulting in the reproduction of prescribed "old" knowledge and the lack of production of "new" knowledge. This might, in the long run, be an example of cultural violence if learner participation in developing the content (including action itself) is denied. It would mean that autonomy and creativity are not rewarded (or are directly or indirectly punished). This again might result in inactive learners without the possibility of engaging themselves in problem solving.

Peace education projects introduced in such situations might place special emphasis upon changing the educational form. Important goals might be to encourage the participation of the students in decision making about both form and content. In this sense, education for peace is more a question of method or forms of communication than of content, that is, it would center on the solution of problems in which participants are engaged. Which problems are selected is highly dependent upon the subjective viewpoints of the participants themselves, and this would mean that the content of peace education would vary greatly depending on the group's social, political, economic and cultural situation.

ORGANIZATIONAL STRUCTURE

The formal educational system in most countries is characterized by the following: the division of knowledge into specific subjects; teachers with specific competencies in these subjects; the grouping of students into classes; and the division of time into periods and breaks. These basic characteristics (others could be added) are important structural components, which allow for only certain types of initiatives for introducing peace education into the curriculum. Thus, it is possible to change the content of a specific subject in such a way that it would deal more with the subject of peace. Such change in the content might not have any significance for the other components such as the methods employed, the division of knowledge into subjects and the division of time into periods and breaks.

If, however, the form of education is regarded as a problem, as well as the way knowledge has been divided into subjects, the peace educator runs into other problems of a structural nature, that is, the peace education project might contradict the basic characteristics of the structure in which it is introduced. If, for instance, a peace education project is based on the principles of problem orientation and participatory decision making, it could not, without problems, be introduced into a school system which rigidly practices the division into subjects, classes, and periods.

It would be extremely difficult to realize problem-oriented and participatory education through a prescribed plan for a subject, carried out by a teacher in a rigidly-structured classroom situation with 30 students, in periods of 45 minutes each. Apart from the rigidity imposed by these three components (subject, class, time), the greatest barrier for peace education projects might be the rules laid down in educational systems concerning evaluation of the students, through which students are sorted into categories according to their achievement in terms of grades (this is not the place to discuss the sorting function of the school and its role in the reproduction of inequalities in society).

Through this discussion about organizational structure, it should be clear that a peace education project might be in harmony or disharmony with it. Therefore, it is possible that so many disharmonies exist that the structure itself must be changed before peace education can be introduced. The question then arises whether the organizational structure can be changed through changes in form and content, or whether this is impossible until changes are brought about in the society which has produced an educational structure antagonistic to problem orientation and dialogue.

CONCLUSION

This essay has discussed peace education in terms of content, form, and organizational structure. It has been argued that peace education involves the principles of problem orientation (content) and participatory decision-making (dialogical form). These two principles need to be implemented at the same time because one implies the other. Therefore, projects focusing on only one of the two will necessarily have an unintended effect on the other as well. If such projects are feasible, it means that the rules laid down in the structure are such that a possibility exists for dialogue. If such projects are met with repression, however, the structural rules regulating education are anti-dialogical in nature, and therefore may not be changed from within the system. Then the question arises as to how the educational system can be altered through a change in society as such.

Some peace educators claim that societal change in the direction of more justice cannot come from within the school itself. This would mean that education for peace would mainly have to occur outside of school, through the action of the adult population. Such conscientization efforts would create political forces, which would be instrumental in the struggle for social justice on the global as well as local levels, including changes in the formal educational system. Whether or not education for peace is attempted within or outside the school, however, it seems that unless it becomes part of the overall process of nonviolent social change, it will not succeed in contributing to the creation of peace and social justice.

Finally, I would like the reader to note that I have discussed the three components separately in this essay. This strong classification is made for purpose of analysis only. It is very important to analyze the mutual relationships between the three components by posing the following questions: How would the selected content influence the communication forms? How could the selected communication form influence the development of content? What is the impact of the organizational structure (including curriculum plans) upon content selection and the choice of communication form? What may be the impact of educational activities upon future structural and organizational patterns?

REFERENCES

UNESCO. (1974). *Recommendation concerning education for international understanding, co-operation and peace and education relating to human rights and fundamental freedoms.* Paris, France: UNESCO. (Recommendation adopted by the General Conference of UNESCO at the 18th session, on November 19, 1974)

CHAPTER 8

THE MORAL AND SPIRITUAL FOUNDATIONS OF PEACE EDUCATION

Dale T. Snauwaert

INTRODUCTION

Does the use of military force require moral justification, or is political necessity sufficient? Can the use of force ever be morally justified? If yes, what principles justify and govern its use? Are there certain things that never should be done to another human being? Are there things that must be provided to every human being? Is peace a basic right? Does peace not only involve the absence of direct violence (negative peace), but also include the absence of structural violence—injustice—(positive peace) as well? Should citizens of a democracy be educated in order to participate in ethical and political discourse concerning these questions?

MORALITY, POLITICS, AND PEACE EDUCATION

Political realism, arguably the leading theory of international relations, denies the existence of morality in relations between nations and peoples.

Encyclopedia of Peace Education, pp. 67–73
Copyright © 2008 by Information Age Publishing
All rights of reproduction in any form reserved.

It maintains that these relations are *purely political,* in the sense that they exclusively concern national-interests and power, not what is right or good per se (Doyle, 1997; Mapel, 1996; McMahan, 1996; Smith, 1986). Realism does posit the existence of a moral community existing within the boundaries of the nation-state. There exists a national interest, a common good, which state agents are obligated to enhance. There is also a moral imperative to provide an umbrella of security for the people of the nation. Officials of the state are morally obligated to pursue the national interest and the security of the people through the prudent exercise of power, including the deployment of military force. This view, however, is morally exclusionary—it posits that human beings existing outside one's nation are not members of one's national moral community and thus do not require moral consideration. Ethics stop at the border. In contrast, peace education is premised upon the cosmopolitan belief that the moral community includes all human beings, that all human beings have moral standing, and thus war and peace, justice and injustice, are global moral considerations. It is not merely a philosophical ideal, for there is an "actually existing cosmopolitanism," a transnational, global moral community based on widespread agreement (Bobbio, 1990/1996; Bok, 1995; Boulding, 1988; Brown, 1992; Buergentahl, 1995; Cooper, 1999; Corcoran, 2005; Dalai-Lama, 1999; Falk, 1989; R. A. Falk, 2000; Finnis, 1980; Glover, 2000; Hayden, 2001; Held, 1995; Kant, 1795/1983; Kung, 1993; Kung & Kuschel, 1993b; Maritain, 1958; Nussbaum, 1996; Perry, 1998).

At its core, morality concerns the question: *How should we live?* This is a question concerning the good life, and it constitutes a *eudaimoniac* perspective (Aristotle, 1965). The Greek word *eudaimonia* is often translated as happiness, but a more accurate translation is human fulfillment, well-being, and/or flourishing. The fundamental presupposition of this ethical perspective is that human beings seek fulfillment in terms of the enjoyment of an integrated set of basic goods (health, knowledge, friendship, aesthetic experience, play, work, sustainable environment, etc.) that together constitute human flourishing. From this perspective, individuals have a "human right" to these basic goods (Finnis, 1980). As Henry Shue (1980) suggests: "A moral right provides (1) the rational basis for a justified demand and (2) that the actual enjoyment of a substance be (3) socially guaranteed against standard threats" (p. 13). From this perspective, rights are justified demands for the enjoyment of goods, which are guaranteed by the society. Rights thus define what the individual is due, is justified in demanding, and/or is protected from. In this way, rights are moral and legal devices which define the moral and, when codified in law, legal boundaries of human relationships. Rights define what choices can never be made or those that must be made. Human rights to basic goods in turn evoke correlative duties, which are basic moral obligations required for basic rights:

(a) positive duties of mutual care and support (duty to aid);
(b) negative duties of no harm to others (duty to avoid harm);
(c) norms of rudimentary fairness (duty to protect) (Bok, 1995; Shue, 1980).

The moral equation is not merely about what the individual is due, but also, it fundamentally involves what individuals are obligated to provide or refrain from in relation to others. The duty to *avoid* harm entails restraint, the obligation to refrain from destructive action. The duty to *protect* entails the responsibility for establishment of norms, social practices, and institutions that enforce the duty to avoid deprivation. The duty to *aid* is positive in the sense that it is on obligation to *provide* for those in need. If individuals have a right to pursue happiness, to pursue human fulfillment, then this set of duties *and* their institutionalization are morally imperative on a social level. These correlative duties are necessary for the minimal level of social cooperation necessary for human flourishing.

Does this imperative apply to the level of foreign relations? This question can be rephrased in terms of moral duty. There is an important distinction between "positional" duty and "natural" duty. Positional duty constitutes obligations that are entailed by a particular position or role in the society. Positional duties relate to special relationships connected to specific roles. Natural duty refers to obligations that are owed to all human beings regardless of position or specialized relationships. Natural duties speak to obligations that human beings possess and owe each other *as* human beings. Are the basic duties, the common values above, positional or natural? Do they apply to relations between societies and peoples? The claim that human beings have a right to pursue happiness, including rights to all goods necessary for human flourishing, is based upon the presupposition that human beings possess intrinsic value, that they are ends. It is an ethic that proclaims the sovereignty, not of any temporal governmental power, but that of human dignity. Human dignity is not defined by political borders but establishes a global, cosmopolitan moral community. The proposition here is that membership in the moral community is based upon the recognition of the intrinsic value of innate human characteristics and capacities. Peace, therefore, can be defined as a cosmopolitan moral order that secures human rights and duties necessary for human flourishing.

When human rights are threatened or violated on a mass scale, such as aggressive war and genocide, the "just war" tradition maintains that the aggrieved party has a right to protect itself and to restore a just peace, and others, friends and allies, are justified in intervening to protect or restore that peace. This intervention can entail a justified use of force. The obligation to act for the protection of a just peace is founded upon a right of self-defense and an obligation to help others in need. In its efforts to defend a just peace, just war theory has developed two sets of principled considerations that define the standards for moral decision making concerning both the decision to go to war and the right conduct of war: *jus ad bellum* and *jus in bello* respectively. In this moral tradition, there exists a *prima facie* presumption against violence, and thus, the use of force requires moral justification. The moral justifiability of using force is contingent upon meeting all of the following criteria: just cause, right authority, right intention, proportionality, reasonable hope of success, and last resort. *Jus in bello* pertains to the right conduct of force. From this perspective, the use of force must be proportional and consistent with noncombatant immunity—the principles of proportionality and discrimination respectively. The use of force may be morally justified to restore a just peace, but it can never fall into total war, for then it contradicts its own justification, the protection of human dignity (Allen, 1991/2001; Bishops, 1983/1992; Boyle, 1996; Cady, 1989; Finnis, 1996; Ford, 1970; Hoffman, 1981; Holmes, 1989, 1989/1992; Nardin, 1996; Ramsborth & Tom. 1996; Ramsey, 1961, 1968/1983; Turner Johnson, 1981, 1999; Walzer, 1970, 1997; Wasserstrom, 1970; Yoder, 1984).

Peace, as a cosmopolitan moral order, is in turn contingent upon the capacity of individual persons to respond to the inherent dignity, the intrinsic value of others. Principles of rights and duties are essential, but they remain powerless without the internal moral resources that equip one to morally respond to others.

There are two basic moral sensibilities that form our moral capacity: "I can't" and "I must" (Fromm, 1947; Glover, 2000). "I can't" constitutes the capacity to refrain from doing harm—a capacity of restraint. It is grounded in the capacity of internal reflection and self-awareness of what is consistent with one's own integrity (Arendt, 1971, 1992, 1994; Arendt & Kohn, 2003; Dalai-Lama, 1999; Hanh, 1987). It is based upon the moral perspective that it is "better to suffer wrong than to do wrong." In Plato's *Gorgias*, Socrates states metaphorically:

> it would be better for me that my lyre or a chorus I direct should be out of tune and loud with discord, and that multitudes of men should disagree with me rather than I, being one, should be out of harmony with myself and contradict me. (Arendt & Kohn, 2003, p. 181)

In other words, if I harm others, then I will not be able to live with my self. The potential internal discord stops me. It is an internal, spiritual mechanism of restraint.

"I must" constitutes the capacity to positively respond, with care and compassion, to the needs of others. This response requires the capacity to meet the other as a subject, as an end. It is based in the recognition of the intrinsic value of the other person (Buber, 1970). It also involves the awareness of the interdependence and interconnection between human beings. It also entails the capacity of equanimity, the ability to remain impartial while being able to take the perspective of the other (Dalai-Lama, 1999).

CONCLUSION

From this perspective, morality and thereby, peace, is structured in the overall quality of our hearts and minds (Dalai-Lama, 1999). As Betty Reardon maintains, peace education should aim at the transformation of both the structures of society *and* the structures of consciousness (Reardon, 1988). These points suggest that peace education has interrelated moral *and* spiritual foundations.

REFERENCES

Allen, J. L. (2001). *War: A primer for Christians*. Dallas, TX: First Maguire Center/ Southern Methodist University Press. (Original work published 1991)

Arendt, H. (1971). *The life of the mind* (Vol. 1). New York: Harcourt.

Arendt, H. (1992). Lectures on Kant's political philosophy. In R. Beiner (Ed.), *Hannah Arendt lectures on Kant's political philosophy* (pp. 3-88). Chicago: The University of Chicago Press.

Arendt, H. (1994). *Eichmann in Jerusalem: A report on the banality of evil*. New York: Penguin Books.

Arendt, H., & Kohn, J. (2003). *Responsibility and judgment* (1st ed.). New York: Schocken Books.

Aristotle. (1965). *Nicomachean ethics* (J. A. K. Thomson, Trans.). Baltimore, MD: Penguin Books.

Bishops, U. S. C. (1992). The challenge of peace: God's promise and our response. In J. B. Elshtain (Ed.), *Just war theory* (pp. 77-168). New York: New York University Press. (Original work published 1983)

Bobbio, N. (1996). *The age of rights*. Cambridge, England: Polity Press. (Original work published 1990)

Bok, S. (1995). *Common values*. Columbia, MO: University of Missouri Press.

Boulding, E. (1988). *Building a global civic culture: Education for an interdependent world*. New York: Teachers College Press.

Boyle, J. (1996). Just war thinking in catholic natural law. In T. Nardin (Ed.), *The ethics of war and peace: Religious and secular perspectives* (pp. 40-53). Princeton, NJ: Princeton University Press.

Brown, C. (1992). *International relations theory: New normative approaches.* New York: Columbia University Press.

Buber, M. (1970). *I and thou* (W. Kaufman, Trans.). New York: Scribners.

Buergentahl, T. (1995). *International human rights.* St. Paul, MN: West.

Cady, D. L. (1989). *From warism to pacifism: A moral continuum.* Philadelphia, PA: Temple University Press.

Cooper, B. (Ed.). (1999). *War crimes: The legacy of Nuremberg.* New York: TV Books.

Corcoran, P. B. (Ed.). (2005). *The earth charter in action: Toward a sustainable world.* Amsterdam, the Netherlands: KIT Publishers, in cooperation with the Earth Charter Initiative, San Jose, Costa Rica.

Dalai-Lama. (1999). *Ethics for the new millennium.* New York: Riverhead Books.

Doyle, M. W. (1997). *Ways of war and peace.* New York, NY: W.W. Norton.

Falk, R. (1989). *Revitalizing international law.* Ames, IA: Iowa State University Press.

Falk, R. A. (2000). *Human rights horizons: The pursuit of justice in a globalizing world.* New York: Routledge.

Finnis, J. (1980). *Natural law and natural rights.* Oxford, England: Clarendon Press.

Finnis, J. (1996). The ethics of war and peace in the catholic natural law tradition. In T. Nardin (Ed.), *The ethics of war and peace: Religious and secular perspectives* (pp. 15-37). Princeton, NJ: Princeton University Press.

Ford, J. C. (1970). The morality of obliteration bombing. In R. A. Wasserstrom (Ed.), *War and morality* (pp. 15-41). Belmont, CA: Wadsworth.

Fromm, E. (1947). *Man for himself: An inquiry into the psychology of ethics.* New York: Rinehart & Company.

Glover, J. (2000). *Humanity: A moral history of the twentieth century.* New Haven, CT: Yale University Press.

Hanh, T. N. (1987). *Being peace.* Berkeley, CA: Parallax Press.

Hayden, P. (Ed.). (2001). *The philosophy of human rights.* St. Paul, MN: Paragon House.

Held, D. (1995). *Democracy and the global order.* Stanford, CA: Stanford University Press.

Hoffman, S. (1981). *Duties beyond borders: On the limits and possibilities of ethical international politics.* Syracuse, NY: Syracuse University Press.

Holmes, R. L. (1989). *On war and morality.* Princeton, NJ: Princeton University Press.

Holmes, R. L. (1992). Can war be morally justified? The just war theory. In J. B. Elshtain (Ed.), *Just war theory* (pp. 195-233). New York: New York University Press. (Original work published 1989)

Kant, I. (1983). *Perpetual peace and other essays* (T. Humphrey., Trans.). Cambridge, MA: Hackett. (Original work published 1795)

Kung, H. (1993a). *Global responsibility: In search of a new world ethic.* New York: Continuum.

Kung, H., & Kuschel, J.-K. (Ed.). (1993b). *A global ethic: The declaration of the parliament of the world's religions.* New York: Continuum.

Mapel, D. R. (1996). Realism and the ethics of war and peace. In T. Nardin (Ed.), *The ethics of war and peace: Religious and secular perspectives* (pp. 54-77). Princeton, NJ: Princeton University Press.

Maritain, J. (1958). *The rights of man and natural law.* London, UK: Geoffrey Bles.

McMahan, J. (1996). Realism, morality, and war. In T. Nardin (Ed.), *The ethics of war and peace: Religious and secular perspectives* (pp. 78-92). Princeton, NJ: Princeton University Press.

Nardin, T. (Ed.). (1996). *The ethics of war and peace: Religious and secular perspectives.* Princeton, NJ: Princeton University Press.

Nussbaum, M. (1996). *For love of country: Debating the limits of patriotism.* Boston: Beacon Press.

Perry, M. J. (1998). *The idea of rights: Four inquiries.* New York: Oxford University Press.

Ramsborth, O., & Tom, W. (1996). *Humanitarian intervention in contemporary conflict: A reconceptualization.* Cambridge, England: Polity Press.

Ramsey, P. (1961). *War and the Christian conscience: How shall modern war be conducted justly?* Durham, NC: Duke University Press.

Ramsey, P. (1983). *The just war: Force and political responsibility.* New York: University Press of America. (Original work published 1968)

Reardon, B. (1988). *Comprehensive peace education: Educating for global responsibility.* New York: Teachers College Press.

Shue, H. (1980). *Basic rights: Subsistence, affluence, and U.S. Foreign policy.* Princeton, NJ: Princeton University Press.

Smith, M. J. (1986). *Realist thought from Weber to Kissinger.* Baton Rouge, LA: Louisiana State University Press.

Turner Johnson, J. (1981). *Just war tradition and the restraint of war: A moral and historical inquiry.* Princeton, NJ: Princeton University Press.

Turner Johnson, J. (1999). *Morality and contemporary warfare.* New Haven, CT: Yale University Press.

Walzer, M. (1970). Moral judgment in time of war. In R. A. Wasserstrom (Ed.), *War and morality* (pp. 54-62). Belmont, CA: Wadsworth.

Walzer, M. (1997). *Just and unjust wars: A moral argument with historical illustrations.* New York: Basic Books.

Wasserstrom, R. A. (1970). On the morality of war: A preliminary inquiry. In R. A. Wasserstrom (Ed.), *War and morality* (pp. 78-101). Belmont, CA: Wadsworth.

Yoder, J. H. (1984). *When war is unjust: Being honest in just-war thinking.* Minneapolis, MN: Augsburg.

CHAPTER 9

THE UNITED NATIONS
AND PEACE EDUCATION

James S. Page

DEFINITIONS

The United Nations (UN) is a global intergovernmental organization established on October 24, 1945 with the general aims of maintaining international peace and encouraging international cooperation. The UN refers to the overarching organization, although specialist UN agencies and forums have been established to further specific objectives. With some exceptions, UN declarations and instruments constitute so-called soft law, which is to say that they work through the power of moral persuasion. Since international peace and co-operation are central to the founding principles of the UN, it is logical that, within the official declarations and instruments of the UN, one ought to find formulations regarding peace education. Further, in seeking to understand peace education, it is logical that we ought to be aware of these formulations including their strengths and weaknesses.

Encyclopedia of Peace Education, pp. 75–83
Copyright © 2008 by Information Age Publishing
All rights of reproduction in any form reserved.

THE UN CHARTER AND
THE UNIVERSAL DECLARATION OF HUMAN RIGHTS

The charter of the UN specifically outlines the purpose of the organization as that of preventing future war. Peace education is one crucial means by which this aim can be fulfilled. The preamble to the charter contains a reference to "reaffirm faith in the ... dignity and worth of the human person" and to "establish conditions under which justice and respect" for international obligations can be maintained (UN, 1945). It is difficult to see the tasks of establishing or reaffirming faith in the dignity of the human person or establishing respect for international obligations without involving education. The other fundamental recognition of peace education lies within the Universal Declaration of Human Rights. Article 26 declares: "Education shall be directed ... to the strengthening of respect for human rights and fundamental freedoms. It shall promote understanding, tolerance and friendship ... and shall further the activities of the United Nations for the maintenance of peace" (United Nations General Assembly [UNGA], 1948).

UNESCO AND PEACE EDUCATION

The agency within the UN system that has pre-eminent responsibility for education and educational policy is the United Nations Educational, Scientific and Cultural Organization (UNESCO), and thus, it would be expected that this international organization would have the most to say about peace education. In fact, peace education is central to the constitutional mandate of UNESCO: the preamble to its constitution (1945) commences by noting that, as war begins in the minds of individuals, so too should the defenses against war be constructed in the minds of individuals. Indeed, most of the declarations within the Preamble deal expressly with either building peace or preventing war. UNESCO shares with other UN organizations a fundamental commitment to international peace, but is unique in its mandate to operate through the mediums of education, science, and culture. If we ignore the preamble, it could be argued that the commitment of UNESCO to peace education within its 1945 constitution is only implied. However, since that time, there have been a number of more explicit commitments by UNESCO to peace education, namely in 1974, 1980, 1995, and, most recently through the UNESCO commitment to the "culture of peace" programs, which will be discussed in further detail below.

One specific activity of UNESCO in encouraging peace education is the Associated Schools Project Network (ASPnet), founded in 1953, and currently involving a network of some 7,900 educational institutions in 176 countries. ASPnet is committed to the UNESCO objectives of encouraging peace and international understanding, although it is noteworthy that this commitment has become more open, with, for instance, a commitment by ASPnet to the "four pillars of education," as outlined in the Delors (1996) report, including the pillars of "learning to know, learning to be, learning to do, and *learning to live together*" (pp. 91-96, emphasis added). The activities of ASPnet espouse peace education principles and include: the linking of schools from different countries, student projects, local and regional networking, international camps, conferences, discussions, campaigns and student competitions, all oriented towards improving the quality of education and towards enhancing respect for other cultures and traditions.

PEACE EDUCATION AND THE RIGHTS OF CHILDREN

The commitment of the UN to peace education is also reflected in the instruments on the rights of the child. The 1959 *Declaration of the Rights of the Child* might be summarized as emphasizing the right that children have to protection and education. The seventh principle expressly states that a child has the right to an education that will develop a sense of moral and social responsibility. As a corollary of this, one could argue that a child has the right to peace education. In the same vein, the 1989 *Convention on the Rights of the Child* Article 29.1 (d) indicates that the education of the child shall be directed to "the preparation of the child for responsible life in a free society, in the spirit of understanding, peace, tolerance, equality of the sexes, and friendship among all peoples, ethnic, national and religious groups and person of indigenous origin." Given the importance of peace and peace education for children, it is not surprising that peace education figures prominently in promotional literature from the United Nations Children's Fund (UNICEF), although UNICEF's emphasis on peace education mostly concerns postconflict situations. It is also not surprising that in 1996, UNICEF adopted peace education as part of its antiwar agenda.

One of the general observations one might make regarding UN international instruments dealing with peace education is that they have become gradually more assertive in terms of rights and expectations. This is evident with the 2002 document *A World Fit for Children*, which was adopted unanimously by the UNGA. In Article 5, "a world fit for children" is described as one of sustainable development "founded upon principles of democracy, equality, non-discrimination, peace and social justice and the universality, indivisibility, interdependence and

interrelatedness of all human rights, including the right to development"
(UNGA, 2002b). Much of the document focuses upon the right of
children to protection from harm and violence. However, an important
section deals with the challenge of providing quality education. Within
Article 40, the signatories to this document indicate that they will
implement a range of strategies and actions, including, at point 40.7,
strategies and actions which will

> ensure that education programmes and materials reflect fully the promo-
> tion and protection of human rights and the values of peace, tolerance and
> gender equality, using every opportunity presented by the International
> Decade for a Culture of Peace and Non-Violence for the Children of the
> World, 2001-2010. (UNGA, 2002b)

Clearly this is a forthright commitment to peace education.

THE UN AND DISARMAMENT EDUCATION

The UN has long held a commitment to disarmament education,
generally perceived to be an element within peace education. In 1978,
the 10th general session of the UNGA (1978) was devoted entirely to
disarmament, and is thus generally known as the Special Session on
Disarmament I or simply SSOD I. Articles 106 and 107 of the *Final
Document* specifically urged governments and international
organizations to develop programs in disarmament and peace
education at all levels, and indicated that disarmament education ought
to be included within formal curricula. In 1980, UNESCO convened the
World Congress on Disarmament Education, as promised in the
previous SSOD I. *The Final Document and Report of the Congress* is
noteworthy in that disarmament education is posited as being an
essential component of peace education, involving how to think, rather
than what to think, and is also linked with development and equity
issues. Importantly, the *Final Document and Report* indicated that the
commitment to disarmament education should be manifest throughout
curricula at all levels of education.

In 1982, the UNGA held the Special Session on Disarmament II
(SSOD II), the centerpiece of which was the World Disarmament
Campaign, lasting from 1982 to 1992. The World Disarmament
Campaign might be described as an exercise to mobilize popular support
for disarmament and was thus linked very much to the efforts of the peace
movement and of the work of nongovernment organizations. The
campaign might be also described as an effort in nonformal peace
education, in that the aim was to educate people about the importance of

disarmament, although the mechanism for doing this was generally outside of formal educational institutions. Edith Ballantyne and Felicity Hill (2001) have suggested that it remains an open question as to whether the campaign was successful. Major limitations were a lack of funding and the inherent problems with saying anything that might imply specific criticism of UN member states. One could argue that the campaign was not a success, in that disarmament during the following decade was minimal. However, one could also argue that the pressure leading to the end of the Cold War was part of the general consciousness-raising engendered by the campaign.

In 1992, the World Disarmament Campaign was converted into a permanent organization, namely the United Nations Disarmament Program, which was perhaps a tacit admission of failure. If the campaign had been truly successful, then the process of creating a permanent agency would hardly have been necessary. Nevertheless, throughout the 1990s, the UNGA made periodic statements on the importance of disarmament education. In 2000, the UNGA called for the secretary-general, with the assistance of experts, to produce a study on disarmament and nonproliferation education. In 2002, the study was presented and accepted by the UNGA. The resulting document, *The United Nations Study on Disarmament and Non-proliferation Education*, is an important international document that confirms the international commitment to peace education. Notably, the document gives a prescriptive definition and list of the objectives of disarmament and non-proliferation education, within Articles 6-0. The authors summarize the province of such education in Article 20, in that such education is "a base of theoretical and practical knowledge, [which] allows individuals to choose for themselves values that reject violence, resolve conflicts peacefully and sustain a culture of peace" (UNGA, 2002a).

PEACE EDUCATION AS A HUMAN RIGHT

One of the interesting developments in the thinking of the UN has been the meshing of peace education and human rights education. The *Vienna Declaration and Programme of Action* of the 1993 World Conference on Human Rights in Vienna, at Part 2, paragraphs 78-82, sees peace education as being part of human rights education and human rights education as crucial for world peace. The Vienna conference was organized by the UN and the declaration subsequently published by the UNGA. More recently, peace educators such as Betty Reardon (1997, 2000) have warmed to this idea of peace education as a right. Indeed, if peace is a human right, it is not something that we merely hope for, but rather, as Douglas Roche (2003) forcefully puts it, something we demand. Further, peace education, in this perspective, also becomes what we ought to demand as a right, rather than an altruistic addition to the educational endeavor.

The conception of peace education as a human right thus flows very much from seeing peace itself as a human right. The UN enunciated this view in a brief yet powerful document, *Declaration on the Rights of Peoples to Peace*, UNGA Resolution 39/11, adopted by the UNGA on November 12, 1984. Interestingly, most Western nations abstained from voting on this resolution and on a similar resolution, 2 years later, expressing a right to development. Nevertheless, the above declaration still has the status of being an officially adopted instrument of the UN. The connection between the right of peace and right to peace education is quite a straightforward one. If peace is to be regarded as a right, then people therefore should have the right to be educated and informed about that right, as any particular right is rendered meaningless if individuals and societies are not informed that they have it.

THE UN AND EDUCATION FOR TOLERANCE

Within UN programs on education for tolerance, there are also numerous commitments to peace education. The year 1995 was designated as the United Nations Year for Tolerance, with UNESCO as the lead agency. The UNESCO *Declaration of Principles on Tolerance* (1995) and the UNGA make it clear that tolerance is an essential requirement for peace. Article 1 of the UNESCO document goes so far as to describe tolerance as the virtue which makes peace possible and which contributes to the replacement of a culture of violence by a culture of peace. The UNESCO document also makes specific reference within Article 4 to the importance of education. Education is the most effective means for preventing intolerance and the initial step is informing people what their rights and freedoms are. Education for tolerance should encourage development of independent judgment, critical thinking and ethical reasoning skills. Interestingly, Article 4.4 involves a pledge by the signatories to improve teacher training, curricula, textbooks, lessons and educational materials "with a view to educating caring and responsible citizens open to other cultures, able to appreciate the value of freedom, respectful of human dignity and differences, and able to prevent conflicts or resolve them by non-violent means" (UNESCO, 1995). As such, the above statement serves as a useful summary of the aims of peace education.

PEACE EDUCATION AND A CULTURE OF PEACE

The emergence of the emphasis on a culture of peace and education for a culture of peace is part of a wider realization that the attainment of peace is not merely an institutional problem, but rather one that requires the subtle elements of cultural change. The formal commitment of the UN towards a culture of peace can be best understood through a remarkable and ambitious document, the *Declaration and Programme of Action on a Culture of Peace*, UNGA Resolution 53/243, adopted by the UNGA on September 13, 1999. In sum, this instrument reflects the trend to a more integrated understanding of both peace and peace education, encompassing direct, structural and cultural peace. The document also acknowledges that peace must be something that emerges from local sources, rather than being imposed from above. In other words, there needs to be a grassroots movement for a culture of peace.

The year 2000 was designated by the UN as the International Year for a Culture of Peace, and this commitment has been extended with the recognition of the International Decade for a Culture of Peace and Non-Violence for the Children of the World (2001-2010). UNESCO has been the lead agency for the programs associated with a culture of peace. Article A/4 of the *Declaration and Programme of Action on a Culture of Peace* indicates that education is one of the principal means to build a culture of peace, and Article B/9 contains specific actions for fostering a culture of peace through education. Such actions include involving children in activities for instilling the values and goals of a culture of peace, revising of curricula and textbooks with consideration to previous declarations of UNESCO on peace, ensuring equality of access for women, reinvigorating international educational cooperation, encouraging and strengthening efforts by actors involved in developing values and skills conducive to a culture of peace, encouraging the relevant entities of the UN system, and expanding initiatives promoting a culture of peace in institutions of higher education.

CONCLUSIONS

Overall, it seems reasonable to contend that the commitment of the UN to peace education has reflected an evolving awareness of the nature of peace and the peace process itself. The weakness of the UN is that it tends to operate upon a very statocratic paradigm (Galtung, 1986). This is not surprising, given that it is an intergovernmental organization, and peace has therefore often been understood in a limited sense as constituting the absence of violence between nation-states. It is evident, however, that there has been a gradual increase in awareness of the importance of civil and social processes in the encouragement of peace and of the importance of education for a culture of peace. It is also evident that the commitment of the UN to peace education has progressively become more forthright and explicit. Ultimately, what makes the commitment of the UN so important is symbolic: the documents themselves have no coercive power. However, the power they do have, that of moral persuasion, is perhaps the most influential of all, especially if used astutely by peace educators.

REFERENCES

Ballantyne, E., & Hill, F. (2001). Lessons from past UN disarmament education efforts. *Disarmament Forum, 3*, 13-17.

Delors, J. (Chair) (1996). *Learning: The treasure within. Report to UNESCO of the international commission on education for the twenty-first century (The Delors Report)*. Paris: UNESCO.

Galtung, J. (1986). On the anthropology of the United Nations system. In D. Pitt & T. G. Weiss (Eds.), *The nature of United Nations bureaucracies* (pp. 1-22). London: Croom Helm.

Reardon, B. A. (1997). Human rights as education for peace. In G. J. Andrepoulos & R. P. Claude (Eds.), *Human rights education for the twenty-first century* (pp. 255-261). Philadelphia: University of Pennsylvania Press.

Reardon, B. A. (2000). Peace education: A review and projection. In B. Moon, S. Brown, & M. Ben-Peretz (Eds.), *Routledge international companion to education* (pp. 397-425). London: Routledge.

Roche, D. (2003). *The human right to peace*. Toronto, Canada: Novalis.

United Nations. (1945). *Charter of the United Nations and the statue of the International Court of Justice*. New York: United Nations Department of Public Information.

UNESCO. (1945). *Constitution of the United Nations Educational, Scientific and Cultural Organization*. London: United Nations. (Adopted on November 16, 1945)

UNESCO. (1974). *Recommendation concerning education for international understanding, co-operation and peace and education relating to human rights and fundamental freedoms*. Paris: UNESCO. (Recommendation adopted by the General Conference of UNESCO at the 18th session, on November 19, 1974)

UNESCO. (1980). *World Congress on Disarmament Education: Final document and report*. Paris: UNESCO.

UNESCO. (1994/5). *Declaration and integrated framework of action on education for peace, human rights and democracy*. Paris: UNESCO. (Declaration of the 44th session of the International Conference on Education, Geneva, October 1994, endorsed by the General Conference of UNESCO at its 28th session, October-November, 1995)

UNESCO. (1995). *Declaration of principles on tolerance.* Paris: UNESCO. (Adopted by the General Conference of UNESCO on November 16, 1995)

UNICEF. (1989). *Convention on the rights of the child.* New York: UNICEF. (Adopted by the General Assembly resolution 44/25 of November 20, 1989)

United Nations General Assembly. (1948). *Universal declaration of human rights.* New York: United Nations. (Adopted and proclaimed by the General Assembly. Resolution 217A (3) of December 10, 1948)

United Nations General Assembly. (1959). *Declaration on the rights of the child.* New York: United Nations. (Resolution 1386 (14) of November 20, 1959)

United Nations General Assembly. (1978). *Final document of the tenth special session of the United Nations General Assembly (SSODI—Special Session on Disarmament I).* New York: United Nations.

United Nations General Assembly. (1984). *Right of peoples to peace.* New York: United Nations. (Resolution A/RES/39/11)

United Nations General Assembly. (1993). *Vienna declaration and programme of action (World Conference on Human Rights).* New York: United Nations. (A/CONF. 157/23 on June 25, 1993)

United Nations General Assembly. (1995). *International decade for a culture of peace and non-violence for the children of the world (2001-2010).* New York: United Nations. (Resolution A/53/25)

United Nations General Assembly. (1999). *Declaration and programme of action on a culture of peace.* New York: United Nations. (Resolution A/53/243)

United Nations General Assembly. (2000). *International decade for a culture of peace and non-violence for the children of the world: Report of the Secretary-General.* New York: United Nations. (Reference A/55/377)

United Nations General Assembly. (2002a). *United Nations study on disarmament and non-proliferation education.* New York: United Nations. (Resolution A/57/124)

United Nations General Assembly. (2002b). *A world fit for children.* New York: United Nations. (Adopted by the General Assembly. (Resolution S-27/2 on May 10, 2002)

SECTION III

Core Concepts in Peace Education

Having examined some foundational ideas about the moral foundations, form, and structure of peace education, it is important now to shift our focus towards core concepts that have shaped the field of peace education. Whether emphasizing human rights, international development, environmental awareness, multiculturalism, conflict resolution, or disarmament, peace education research and practice are united by certain concepts and principles. These concepts are not the only ones that exist, nor are they fixed as scholars continue to contribute to shaping how these concepts are constructed and utilized in peace education. It is important to note that an analysis of gender underscores all of the areas discussed in this section. The four chapters that follow in this section discuss caring, sexism/militarism, human rights, and global citizenship—all areas that have received and deserve considerable attention as organizing principles of peace education.

Encyclopedia of Peace Education, pp. 85–86
Copyright © 2008 by Information Age Publishing
All rights of reproduction in any form reserved.

QUESTIONS FOR CONSIDERATION

- What unifying elements exist in the field of peace education that provide shared understandings across diverse contexts? What concepts are contextual and vary based on location?
- What is the relationship among peace, justice, and human rights? What values and skills are needed for the achievement of these ideals?
- What is the role of the educator in peace education? What components would teacher training for peace education consist of?

CHAPTER 10

CARING AND PEACE EDUCATION

Nel Noddings

Care theory and peace education go well together. Care theory displaces the lonely, principled moral agent at the heart of traditional ethics with a dyadic relation—"carer" and "cared-for." As human beings, we are inevitably in relation, and our very individuality arises in relation. In every facet of life, we encounter the living other. As Martin Buber (1958/ 1970) put it, "All actual life is encounter" (p. 62). Care theory describes caring encounters and caring relations, and gives us some guidance on how to establish, maintain, and enhance such relations. To teach for caring relations is to teach for peace in communities, in individual lives, and in the world.

ELEMENTS OF CARE THEORY

Care theory begins with a description of the caring relation, one to which both carer and cared-for contribute (Noddings, 1984/2003). The carer (or one-caring) is first of all attentive; she or he listens to the cared-for and is especially attentive to the needs expressed. Simone Weil (1977) said of

Encyclopedia of Peace Education, pp. 87–91

this form of attention, "the soul empties itself of all its own contents in order to receive into itself the being it is looking at" (p. 51). This receptive attention is accompanied by *motivational displacement*, that is, the carer's motivating energy flows toward the expressed needs and projects of the cared-for. Then the carer must do something and respond in some way. In the simplest caring encounters, the need of the cared-for may be met quickly and easily. In other cases, there may be multiple encounters, requiring commitment over time. A relationship over time may be characterized as *caring*, if most of the encounters that make it up are *caring encounters*.

To complete a caring encounter or relation, the cared-for must respond in some way that acknowledges the effort of the carer. This response might be an explicit expression of gratitude, but it could be as simple as an infant's smile, a patient's sigh of relief, or a student's energetic pursuit of an approved project. Without such a response from the cared-for, there is no caring relation despite the best efforts of the carer. Care theory may be unique among moral theories in its recognition of the cared-for's contribution to moral life. We need not give moral credit to the infant for his smile, or to the patient for his sigh, or to the student for his display of energy. Moral credit is not the point. The point is to identify and encourage modes of response that make it possible to establish, maintain, or enhance caring relations.

In mature relationships, we expect that caring relations will be marked by equality or mutuality; that is, we expect that the two members of the relation will regularly exchange places, that is, each takes turns acting as carer and cared-for. When this does not happen, relationships tend to deteriorate.

But many relationships are unequal by their very nature. Relations such as mother-infant, nurse-patient, and teacher-students are necessarily unequal. The infant cannot take a turn as carer, and a patient cannot do for the nurse what the nurse does for the patient. Similarly, the teacher-student relationship is unequal. If the inequality is removed, the relationship may be converted to friendship.

Even under unequal conditions, however, the caring relation is characterized by reciprocity. Both carer and cared-for contribute distinctively to the relation. Clearly, this reciprocity is not contractual; the carer contributes *as* carer, the cared-for *as* cared-for. Those who regularly act as carer in unequal relations are keenly aware of how dependent they are on the response of the cared-for—on the child, the patient, the student, the client. Without that response of acknowledgement, there is a real danger of burnout in the work of caring.

A basic requirement in caring relations is dialogue. It is through dialogue that we come to know one another, and it is in dialogue that needs are expressed. Without dialogue, those who want to care—those who have the best interests of the cared-for at heart—must work with inferred needs (Noddings, 2002). Sometimes, the use of inferred needs is a choice. A parent may decide, without talking with her child, that she knows what the child needs. Similarly, a teacher may infer needs for all fifth graders or all math students (Noddings, 2007). In such cases, conscientious parents and teachers may fail repeatedly to establish caring relations because they have not received what-is-there in the other. The identification of expressed needs through dialogue is crucial at every level of human interaction, and the use of dialogue is central in peace education as well.

EDUCATING FOR PEACE

Peace educators often put considerable emphasis on learning through textbooks, lectures, films, and stories (Noddings, 2005). Such acquisition of cultural knowledge is essential, but it can also be misleading. Students of all ages sometimes suppose that, as a result of such learning, they know all about another culture. They are ready to act upon inferred needs, and they neglect to engage the living other in dialogue, thus missing expressed needs and perhaps creating misunderstandings.

When would-be carers on the global level neglect dialogue and expressed needs, they often come across as insensitive, even arrogant. They may also make grave errors in the allocation of resources. The economist, Joseph Stiglitz (2002) charges that well-meaning representatives of developed nations often make mistakes of this sort. From their own framework of values and interests, they infer the needs of others and generously, but mistakenly, set out to meet them. They may infer that a developing nation needs a large dam for electricity, fast food chains, factories for clothing manufacture, or even democracy, when if asked, the nation's citizens might express entirely different needs and perhaps strongly reject those inferred. Stiglitz comments:

> Those whose lives will be affected by the decisions about how globalization is managed have a right to participate in that debate, and they have a right to know how such decisions have been made in the past. (p. xvi)

We must engage in dialogue to identify the needs, motives, and interests of others. We might be astonished to learn that some people prefer an economic system different from capitalism and a social system other than democracy. Through continuous dialogue, we might change their minds, but they might well cause us to modify our own views. We may enter relationships of mutual caring.

For effective peace education, it is not enough to understand others; we must also understand ourselves (Noddings, 2006). This is hard, and peace educators sometimes make the mistake of adopting lovely principles that stand little chance of translation into practice. We often ignore basic realities about human nature. Evolutionary science has produced considerable evidence on the sources and practice of altruism, for example. The more closely related we are to others by blood or family, the more likely we are to respond altruistically. In discussing caring, I have pointed out that caring starts in the inner circle and may or may not spread to outer circles. When it does spread, it is usually through chains of some sort of common interest.

It is also true of almost all of us that, if our inner circle is attacked, we will fight to defend it, even if we believe on principle that the other side is more "right." These features of human relations are not to be celebrated, but they cannot be denied. We have to face these things about ourselves.

It is imperative, then, for caring peace educators to do all we can to prevent the conditions under which groups will be incited to take sides along blood or national lines. Once the lines are drawn, tragedy will inevitably follow at the individual, group, national, or global level. For too many years, we have put emphasis on fighting fairly, on just war, and on humane rules for the treatment of enemies. However, when situations become dire, these rules are put aside. In light of what we know about human allegiances, this emphasis is hopeless. When things get tough for our own people, we will too often do terrible things.

Care theory, then, concentrates on the prevention of physical conflict and the preservation of life (Brock-Utne, 1985; Reardon, 1985; Ruddick, 1989). We must teach our children what it means to establish caring relations and then work patiently to expand the circles of care through chains of common interests. To establish these chains, we must engage in continuous, unconditional dialogue. We can encourage dialogue among engineers, teachers, musicians, carpenters, students, artists, and any other groups whose occupational or social interests suggest a connection. It is essential to establish such dialogue groups between nations that are at risk of becoming enemies (Saunders, 1991). Through such dialogues, the main points of contention are deliberately avoided. Only when, through the appreciation achieved in dialogue and common projects, it has become unthinkable to do physical harm to these living others—only then can the points of conflict be safely addressed. Through continuous dialogue, common projects, and chains of connection, we expand the circles of caring.

REFERENCES

Brock-Utne, B. (1985). *Educating for peace: A feminist perspective.* New York: Pergamon Press.

Buber, M. (1970). *I and thou* (W. Kaufmann, Trans.). New York: Charles Scribner's Sons. (Original work published 1958)

Noddings, N. (2002). *Starting at home: Caring and social policy.* Berkeley, CA: University of California Press.

Noddings, N. (2003). *Caring: A feminine approach to ethics and moral education.* Berkeley, CA: University of California Press. (Original work published 1984)

Noddings, N. (Ed.). (2005). *Educating citizens for global awareness.* New York: Teachers College Press.

Noddings, N.(2006). *Critical lessons: What our schools should teach.* Cambridge, MA: Cambridge University Press.

Noddings, N. (2007). Caring as relation and virtue in teaching. In P. S. Ivanhoe & R. Walker (Eds.), *Working virtue: Virtue ethics and contemporary moral problems* (pp. 41-60). Oxford, England: Oxford University Press.

Reardon, B. (1985). *Sexism and the war system.* New York: Teachers College Press.

Ruddick, S. (1989). *Maternal thinking: Toward a politics of peace.* Boston: Beacon Press.

Saunders, H. (1991). *The other walls.* Princeton, NJ: Princeton University Press.

Stiglitz, J. E. (2002). *Globalization and its discontents.* New York: W. W. Norton.

Weil, S. (1977). *Simone Weil reader* (G. A. Panichas, Ed.). Mt. Kisco, NY: Moyer Bell.

CHAPTER 11

COUNTERING MILITARISM THROUGH PEACE EDUCATION

Carl Mirra

INTRODUCTION

There is no single, uniform definition of militarism, yet scholars have identified some of its common characteristics. In Vagts' (1981) classic study on the history of militarism, he distinguishes it from the "military way." The military way is simply a focused effort to win a particular war with the least amount of bloodshed. Militarism, on the other hand, signifies a range of values, "prestige, actions, and thought associated with armies and wars yet transcending true military purposes ... it may permeate all society and become dominant over all industry and arts" (p. 13). While debate over militaristic attitudes can be traced back to ancient times, the term militarism first appeared in the *Memoirs of Madame de Chastenay* in the early 1800s, according to scholar Werner Conze. In 1869, militarism appeared in a French encyclopedia (Berghahn, 1981).

Contemporary definitions of militarism emphasize that it denotes military domination over political and civic life, thereby posing a threat to representative structures. Johnson (2004) writes that militarism is the

Encyclopedia of Peace Education, pp. 93–97

"phenomenon by which a nation's armed services come to put their institutional preservation ahead of achieving national security [and] the assumption by a nation's armed forces of numerous tasks that should be reserved for civilians" (pp. 23-24). Evans and Newnham (1998) similarly define militarism as the "subordination of civil society to military values" (p. 325). Qualities or values such as hierarchy, obedience, competition and force are exaggerated and revered under militaristic conditions. Militarism, however, is not a precise term as it encompasses ideological and cultural components. Many scholars argue that it entails a value system, whereby the military spirit pervades civil society. A culture of militarism is perpetuated by war toys, video games, movies, and everyday products that celebrate the military and violence (Wahlstrom, 1991). In educational settings, a subtle strand of militarism finds expression not only in the study of warfare, but also in the school system's hierarchal structure and competitive environment where students struggle against others for grades and rewards.

Militarism is frequently associated with nationalist governments and a negative view of human nature. Germany, Italy, and Japan during the 1930s were highly militarized societies that celebrated hierarchy, authority, and the use of force to subdue opponents. Tandon (1989) argued that the slave trade and centuries of European colonialism and neo-colonialism accelerated militarism on the African continent. Militarism was also associated with many Latin American military governments during the 1970s and 1980s, which were called the *seguridad nacional del estado* or the state's national security. Chile, under Augusto Pinochet, and Argentina's junta in this period are examples of militarized governments.

MILITARISM AND PEACE EDUCATION

Of special importance to peace educators is Bacevich's (2005) observation that militarism involves the use of force at the expense of alternative solutions. Following sociologist C. Wright Mills' (1956) description of the "military metaphysic," Bacevich notes that militarism involves the "tendency to see international problems as military problems and to discount the likelihood of finding a solution except through military means" (p. 2). Bacevich locates the rise of militarism in U.S. society at the turn of the twenty-first century, owing principally to the country's inclination to equate national greatness with military prowess. The second Bush administration's doctrines of unilateral and preemptive war also accelerate militarism by prioritizing the use of force.

Militarism need not find expression in warfare alone. War preparedness contributes mightily to militaristic sensibilities. A thriving war industry adds to a militarized world. It is estimated that the major powers alone possess some 30,000 nuclear weapons and global arms spending was roughly U.S.$55.8 billion annually at the turn of the twenty-first century (Menon, 2001). Peace researchers have demonstrated that massive arms spending while human needs are unmet constitute structural violence, since expenditures on arms come at the expense of human needs. Militarism thrives on insecurity, anxiety, and fear, thereby allowing resources to be diverted from education, health care, and related needs. The World Council of Churches has argued that humanity might have avoided the disaster of nuclear war, but not the disaster of malnutrition, educational neglect and lack of health care (Reardon, 1982). These problems are exacerbated by military spending that diverts badly needed resources to excessive military preparedness. This phenomenon is related to the "military-industrial complex," a term coined by U.S. President Dwight Eisenhower in 1961. The president warned that the confluence of the private defense industry with the government led to the "mindless pursuit" of "redundant weapons systems" (Roland, 2001, p. 5). Mills' (1956) formulation of a "power elite" that adopted a military mindset expands Eisenhower's concept to include how economic priorities propel militaristic attitudes.

Peace educators paid particular attention to militarism during the Cold War and its attendant arms race. Disarmament education was offered as an alternative to the rising tide of militarism and war preparations. Following World War II, the Soviet Union, and the United States engaged in an intense rivalry from roughly 1947 to 1991. This period was animated by the threat of nuclear war and war preparedness on a global scale. In 1978, the United Nations Educational, Scientific and Cultural Organization (UNESCO) first promoted "disarmament education" as a remedy to a culture of militarism. The 10th Special Session of the United Nations General Assembly (UNGA) encouraged UNESCO's disarmament education plan, having argued that students must be provided with the tools to "resist propaganda for war and militarism" (UNGA, 1978). UNESCO subsequently held a World Congress on Disarmament Education in 1979. Magnus Haavelsrud, a professor of peace education, collected the Congress' work in an edited volume titled *Approaching Disarmament Education*, which countered "present developments of militarism and suppression" (Haavelsrud, 2004, pp. v, 1-2).

Reardon's (1996) observation that militarism is connected to patriarchy has significantly enhanced the field of peace education in understanding both concepts. She has written that militarism is a "belief system" based on the presupposition that "human beings are by nature violent, aggressive and competitive" (p. 145). Militarism, then, is a value system where civic virtue is conflated with service in the armed forces or more generally with the use of power and force to subdue adversaries. Militarism and sexism are inseparable, Reardon discovered. Galtung's (1996) suggestion that 95% of direct, physical violence is committed by males seems to support Reardon's insistence that militarism and sexism are interrelated. The war system, as Reardon calls it, shares the same core values of patriarchal institutions. Fears of losing control or maintaining dominance are mental frameworks that are common among sexism and militarism. Both patriarchy and the war system exaggerate the qualities of hierarchy, force, coercion, and the preoccupation with protecting oneself against a hostile adversary and/or competitors. According to Reardon, peace educators cannot address the problem of militarism without addressing the problem of sexism.

Peace education aims to reverse the adverse effects of militarism in many ways. The field promotes conflict resolution skills in individuals, schools and international relations as outlined in Reardon and Cabezudo (2002). Moreover, peace researchers have contributed a more balanced view of the human being beyond the militaristic view of human nature as aggressive and hypercompetitive. During the United Nation's International Year of Peace in 1986, leading scientists released "The Seville Statement on Violence." The scientists concluded that, "it is scientifically incorrect to say that war is caused by instinct," and "there are cultures which have not engaged in war for centuries" (Wahlstrom, 1991, pp. 30-31). Grossman (1996) has likewise reported that a U.S. Army study during the World War II discovered that only 15% to 20% of soldiers would fire their weapon. The general who conducted the study concluded that these soldiers possessed an "inner and usually unrealized resistance toward killing" (Grossman, 1996, p. 1). In addition to countering the pessimistic conception of human nature, peace researchers work to highlight the link between the oppression of women and the militaristic spirit that seeks to subjugate perceived enemies.

LOOKING FORWARD

Several organizations have worked to promote a culture of peace for the twenty-first century. UNESCO has sponsored *The International Decade for a Culture of Peace and Non-Violence for the Children of the World (2001 to 2010)*. The Hague Agenda for Peace and Justice (2000) aimed to uncover the root causes of war and militarism, while facilitating peacemaking skills. Redefining human security with regard to environmental and human needs rather than nationalistic imperatives and promoting universal human rights are among the appeal's many initiatives to build a peaceful world. The goals of these various efforts are to replace a culture of militarism with a culture of peace.

REFERENCES

Bacevich, A. (2005). *The new American militarism: How Americans are seduced by war.* Oxford, England: Oxford University Press.

Berghahn, V. (1981). *Militarism: The history of an international debate, 1861-1979.* Cambridge, England: Cambridge University Press.

Evans, G., & Newnham, J. (1998). *The Penguin dictionary of international relations.* London: Penguin Books.

Galtung, J. (1996). *Peace by peaceful Means: Peace and conflict, development and civilization.* London: Sage.

Grossman, D. (1996). *On killing.* New York: Back Bay Books.

Haavelsrud, M. (2004). Target: Disarmament education. *Journal of Peace Education, 1*(1), 37-57.

Johnson, C. (2004). *The sorrows of empire: Militarism, secrecy and the end of the republic.* New York: Henry Holt.

Menon, B. (2001). *Disarmament education: A basic guide.* New York: United Nations/ NGO Committee on Disarmament Affairs.

Mills, C. (1956). *The power elite.* Oxford, England: Oxford University Press.

Reardon, B. (1982). *Militarization, security and peace education: A guide for concerned citizens.* Valley Forge, PA: United Ministries in Education.

Reardon, B. (1996). Militarism and sexism: Influences on education for war. In R. Burns & R. Aspeslagh (Eds.), *Three decades of peace education around the world* (143-160). New York: Garland.

Reardon, B., & Cabezudo, A. (2002). *Learning to abolish war: Teaching toward a culture of peace.* New York: Hague Appeal for Peace.

Roland, A. (2001). *The military-industrial complex.* Washington, DC: American Historical Association.

Tandon, Y. (1989). *Militarism and peace education in Africa: A guide and manual for peace education in Africa.* Nairobi, Kenya: African Association for Literacy Education.

United Nations General Assembly. (1978, June 30). *Final Document of the Tenth Special Session of the General Assembly* (27th session). New York: United Nations.

Vagts, A. (1981). *A history of militarism* (Rev. ed.). Westport, CT: Greenwood Press.

Wahlstrom, R. (1991, March). *Peace education meets the challenge of the cultures of militarism* (Peace Education Miniprints No. 11). Lund University, Sweden: Malmo School of Education.

CHAPTER 12

HUMAN RIGHTS EDUCATION

Felisa Tibbitts

DEFINITION

Human rights education (HRE) is an international movement to promote awareness about the rights accorded by the Universal Declaration of Human Rights (UDHR) and related human rights conventions, and the procedures that exist for the redress of violations of these rights (Amnesty International, 2005; Reardon, 1995; Tibbitts, 1996). Decades ago, the United Nations (UN) and its specialized agencies formally recognized the right of citizens to be informed about the rights and freedoms contained in the documents ratified by their countries—the right to HRE itself (United Nations General Assembly (UNGA), 2005). Since then, numerous policy documents developed by UN-affiliated agencies, international policymaking bodies, regional human rights bodies, and national human rights agencies have referenced HRE, proposing specifically that the treatment of human rights themes should be present in schooling (Pearse, 1987).[1]

The UN Office of the High Commissioner for Human Rights defines HRE as

> training, dissemination and information efforts aimed at the building of a
> universal culture of human rights through the imparting of knowledge and

Encyclopedia of Peace Education, pp. 99–108
Copyright © 2008 by Information Age Publishing

skills and the molding of attitudes directed to: the strengthening of respect for human rights and fundamental freedoms,

(a)   the full development of the human personality and the sense of its dignity,

(b)   the promotion of understanding, tolerance, gender equality and friendship among all nations, indigenous peoples and racial, national, ethnic, religious, and linguistic groups, and

(c)   the enabling of all persons to participate effectively in a free society. (UN, 1996)

This definition is not specific to the schooling sector and in fact, the UN proposes HRE for all sectors of society as part of a "lifelong learning" process for individuals (UN, 1996). The "human rights" to which it refers are broadly defined and include those contained in the UDHR, as well as related treaties and covenants, such as the International Covenant on Economic, Social and Cultural Rights, the International Covenant on Civil and Political Rights, the Convention on the Rights of the Child, and the Convention for the Elimination of All Forms of Discrimination Against Women, among others.[2] Which human rights are addressed in learning situations, and how, has become of increasing interest as the worldwide human rights movement has grown.

THE EXPANSION OF HRE IN SCHOOLS

Although still a developing field, there is increasing evidence that HRE is emerging in the work of nongovernmental organizations (NGOs) at the grassroots level as well as in national systems of education (Buergenthal & Torney, 1976; Claude 1996; Elbers, 2000; Human Rights Education Association (HREA), n.d.; Inter-american Institute Of Human Rights, 2002). The only study focusing on this subject indicated that the number of organizations dedicated to HRE quadrupled between 1980 and 1995, from 12 to 50 (Ramirez, Suarez, & Meyer, 2007). In reality, the numbers are probably much higher since only those organizations that had an Internet presence or were already networked in international circles were documented.

In 2006, an International Bureau of Education (IBE) study that examined the number of times the term "human rights" was mentioned in official documents found a mean of .70, .82, and .64 for countries within the regions of Sub-Saharan Africa, Eastern Europe, the former Union Of Soviet Socialist Republics, Latin American, and the Caribbean, respectively (Ramirez et al., 2007). Interestingly enough, the lowest means were for Asia and Western Europe and North America at .11

(Ramirez et al., 2007), although the range of response rates across regions —from 31% to 74%—suggests that these results are approximate at best. A review in 1996 showed that through the cooperative efforts of NGOs and educational authorities, human rights courses and topics had been introduced into the national curricula in Albania, Australia, Brazil, Canada, Denmark, Norway, the United Kingdom, and Ukraine (Kati & Gjedia, 2003; Tibbitts, 1996). The IBE study and other less formal data suggest that the number of educational systems including human rights in their formal curricula has grown significantly since that time.

Hundreds of human rights-related teaching materials have been developed worldwide for use in classrooms and schools, and many of these are widely available, free of charge, on the Internet. The online resource center of HREA (http://www.hrea.org/index.php?base_id= 101&language_id=1) and other online resource centers serve as good examples. Moreover, bibliographies and descriptive databases of HRE materials are available through key human rights organizations as well as UN-related agencies (Amnesty International, 2005; Council of Europe, n.d.; UNGA, 2005; HREA, n.d.).

During this same period, NGOs which have traditionally spearheaded HRE efforts, also gathered to develop HRE action plans that had an influence on their own work and cooperation with others (Amnesty International, 1996; Netherlands Helsinki Committee, 1996). In the last 5 years, national and regional HRE networks have been established in many parts of the world (HREA, n.d.). In 2005, with the conclusion of the United Nations Decade for Human Rights Education, the office of the UN high commissioner for human rights launched an ongoing and more focused Plan of Action World Program for Human Rights Education (UNGA 2005), which promises to elicit improved cooperation from governments, as well as cross-cutting support from UN bodies (Amnesty International, 2005). The first phase of the world program is focused on promoting HRE in schools.

RATIONALES FOR HRE

The broad normative framework of HRE and the wide spectrum of potential learners have resulted in a great deal of variation in the ways in which HRE has been implemented. Although HRE is defined by the universal framework of international (and sometimes regional) standards, the specific topics and their applications depends upon local and national contexts.

HRE in postconflict or postcolonial countries tends to be associated with the rule of law and authorities trying to establish their legitimacy.

Among groups that experience a high amount of discrimination, and within countries that are highly repressive and undemocratic, HRE tends to be focused on popular empowerment and resistance in relation to these issues. HRE in countries that are democratic but struggling with development can be oriented towards the infusion of human rights principles within sustainable development (Yeban, 2003). In countries that enjoy strong democratic and economic development, HRE is often focused on issues of discrimination, for example in relation to migrants, minorities, or women. Of course, in any country at any given time, HRE can take on different forms and purposes depending upon the context of the program.

Several explanations have been proposed for the increased presence of HRE in schools since the 1990s. One explanation relates to increased globalization, a term still being defined, but recognized as one emphasizing "world citizenship and the strong assumption of personal agency required for global citizenship" (Ramirez et al., 2007, p. 36). Moreover, authorities are increasingly calling on schools to promote respect among peoples, democratic governance, and viable civil societies.

Democratic citizenship, including HRE, has been seen by regional human rights agencies as a way to "manage diversity," with HRE incorporated into processes such as the Graz Stability Pact in South Eastern Europe (Council of Europe, 2001; South House Exchange, 2004). In contemporary Europe, education for democratic citizenship, including HRE, has been seen as a way of promoting young people's active participation in democratic society, in promoting social cohesion and in fighting violence, xenophobia, racism, intolerance, and aggressive nationalism (Froumin, 2003).

In 1978, HRE was already promoted by the United Nations Educational, Scientific, and Cultural Organization (UNESCO) but linked with disarmament (UNESCO, 1978). In 2005, HRE has been linked in intergovernmental circles with a variety of global phenomena, including development and poverty, religious freedom, and globalization in general (UNESCO, 2005). Europe's regional human rights agency, the Council of Europe, is working on developing a "culture of religion" subject that takes an "ethics" and "human rights" based approach to religious teaching. This provides an alternative to governments that currently offer required religion classes that can be a source of division and ethnic nationalism, as in Serbia-Montenegro (Tibbitts, 2003).

NGOs from different countries and regions periodically initiate meetings in which they identify strategies for applying the human rights framework to global challenges. One such symposium, which took place in South Africa in 2001 in a meeting organized in concert with the World

Conference against Racism, identified HRE in schools as a key strategy for combating racism (Flowers, 2001).

PEDAGOGY OF HRE

Since 1995, further elaborations by the UN and other agencies have clarified that HRE has components of knowledge, skills, and attitudes, which should be consistent with recognized human rights principles and which should empower individuals and groups to address oppression and injustice (Amnesty International, 2007; Asia-Pacific Regional Resource Center For Human Rights Education (ARRC), 2003).

HRE has both normative and legal dimensions. The legal dimension incorporates sharing content about international human rights standards as embodied in the UDHR and other treaties and covenants to which countries subscribe. These standards encompass civil and political rights, as well as social, economic, and cultural. In recent years, environmental and collective rights have been added to this evolving framework. This law-oriented approach recognizes the importance of monitoring and accountability in ensuring that governments uphold the letter and spirit of human rights obligations.

At the same time, HRE is a normative and cultural enterprise. The process of HRE is intended to be one that provides skills, knowledge, and motivation to individuals to transform their own lives and realities so that they are more consistent with human rights norms and values. For this reason, interactive, learner-centered methods of are widely promoted. The following kinds of pedagogy are representative of those promoted by HRE advocates. These methods are applicable to all types of HRE but are most comprehensively implemented in adult, popular education learning models.

- *Experiential and activity-centered*: involving the solicitation of learners' prior knowledge and offering activities that draw out learners' experiences and knowledge;
- *Problem-posing*: challenging the learners' prior knowledge;
- *Participative*: encouraging collective efforts in clarifying concepts, analyzing themes and doing the activities;
- *Dialectical*: requiring learners to compare their knowledge with those from other sources;
- *Analytical*: asking learners to think about why things are and how they came to be;

- *Healing*: promoting human rights in intrapersonal and interpersonal relations;
- *Strategic thinking-oriented*: directing learners to set their own goals and to think of strategic ways of achieving them; and
- *Goal and action-oriented*: allowing learners to plan and organize actions in relation to their goals (ARRC, 2003).

HRE in school settings is adapted to the age of learners and the conditions of national/local educational policies and schools. Developmental and conceptual frameworks for HRE have been developed by the UN and several NGOs. These frameworks assist in settings goals for HRE, illustrating both what it shares and what it adds to other educational approaches that address values such as social justice.

Human rights themes and content in school curricula can take the form of cross-cultural themes mandated by educational policy or it can be integrated within existing subjects, such as history, civics/citizenship education, social studies, and humanities. HRE can also be found in arts programs and nonformal clubs and special events that take place in school settings.

In addition to taking place in schools, HRE is often organized in settings of higher education; in training programs for professionals such as the police, prison officials, the military, and social workers; for potentially vulnerable populations such as women and minorities; as part of community development programs; and in public awareness campaigns.

DEVELOPMENTS AND THE FUTURE OF HRE

The HRE field shows signs of continuing development and evolution. At the international level, UN agencies continue to encourage governments to develop formal plans of action for HRE and provide reports on its internal HRE activities as part of regular treaty-based reports. International and national networks of educators, institutes and organizations continue to dialogue and share resources on the content, standards, and methodology of HRE and learning. Research in the field, although currently sparse, is beginning to increase.

Within the educational sector, the human rights normative system is increasingly being proposed as the ethical framework for cultural globalization. Within the human rights sector, the "human rights based approach" that the UN has advocated for all development programming has begun to trickle down to the education sector. Thus, HRE, which has primarily focused on teaching and learning, may eventually be seen as

**Table 12.1.   Methodologies:
Development and Conceptual Framework for HRE**

Levels	Goals	Key Concepts	Specific Human Rights Problems	Education Standards and Instruments
Early Childhood				
Preschool and lower primary- Ages 3-7	Respect for self Respect for parents and teachers Respect for others	Self Community Responsibility	Racism Sexism Unfairness Hurting people (emotionally, physically)	Classroom rules Family life Convention on the Rights of the Child
Later Childhood				
Upper primary- ages 8-11	Social responsibility Citizenship Distinguishing wants from needs from rights	Individual rights Group rights Freedom Equality Justice Rule of law Government Security Democracy	Discrimination/ prejudice Poverty/hunger Injustice Ethnocentricism Passivity	UDHR History of human rights Local, national legal systems Local and national history in human rights terms UNESCO, UNICEF
Adolescence				
Lower secondary ages 12-14	Knowledge of specific human rights	International law World peace World development World political economy World ecology Legal rights Moral rights	Ignorance Apathy Cynicism Political repression Colonialism/ imperialism Economic globalization Environmental degradation	UN Covenants Elimination of racism Elimination of sexism Regional human rights conventions UNHCR NGOs
Older Adolescents and Adults				
Upper secondary ages 15 and up	Knowledge of human rights standards Integration of human rights into personal awareness and behaviors	Moral inclusion/exclusion Moral responsibility/literacy	Genocide Torture	Geneva Conventions Specialized conventions Evolving human rights standards

Source: Flowers, 1998.

part of an overall "human rights based approach" to schooling, which calls attention to overall school culture, policies, and practices related to human rights values.

NOTES

1. During the 1990s, several important international documents on human rights education were elaborated. These were the World Plan of Action on Education for Human Rights and Democracy (Montreal, 1993), the Declaration and Integrated Framework of Action on Education for Peace, Human Rights and Democracy (UNESCO, Paris, 1995), the World Conference on Human Rights (Vienna, 1993), Guidelines for Plans of Action for the United Nations Decade for Human Rights Education 1995-2004 (1995). These refer to the relevant education articles of international treaties and place informal pressure on national governments to cooperate.
2. The full set of human rights documents as well as related general comments can be found on the Web site of the UN Office of the High Commissioner for Human Rights at www.ohchr.org.

RREFERENCES

Amnesty International. (1996). *Human rights education strategy*. Retrieved May 18, 2001, from http://www.amnesty.org/ailib/aipub/1996

Amnesty International. (2005, August 14-20). Human rights education: Building a global culture of human rights. *Developed for 27th International Council Meeting, Circular 25*, 13-14.

Amnesty International. (2007). *What is human rights education?* Retrieved March 17, 2007, from www.amnesty.org

Asia-Pacific Regional Resource Center for Human Rights Education. (2003). What is human rights education. In *Human rights education pack* (pp. 22-23). Bangkok, Thailand: AARC.

Buergenthal, T., & Torney, J. V. (1976). *International human rights and international education*. Washington, DC: U.S. National Commission for UNESCO.

Claude, R. P. (1996). *Educating for human rights: The Philippines and beyond*. Quezon City, Philippines: University of the Philippines Press.

Council of Europe. (2001). *Education for democratic citizenship and management of diversity in Southeast Europe* (DGTV/EDU/CTT: 30). Strasbourg, Austria: Council of Europe.

Council of Europe. (n.d.). *Web site*. Retrieved November 6, 2007, from http://www.coe.int/

Elbers, F. (Ed.). (2000). *Human rights education resource book*. Cambridge, MA: Human Rights Education Associates.

Flowers, N. (Ed.) (1998). *Human rights here and now: Celebrating the Universal Declaration of Human Rights.* Minneapolis, MN: Amnesty International USA and University of Minnesota Human Rights Resource Center.

Flowers, N. (2001, August). *Report.* Unpublished report presented at the Human Rights Education Symposium, Durban, South Africa.

Froumin, I. (2003). *Education for democratic citizenship activities 2001-4. All-European study on policies for education for democratic citizenship (EDC) regional study Eastern Europe Region* (DGIV/EDU/CIT (2003) 28 rev). Strasbourg, Austria: Council of Europe.

Human Rights Education Association. (n.d.) *HREA Web site.* Retrieved November 6, 2007, from http://www.hrea.org/

Inter-American Institute of Human Rights. (2002). *Inter-American report on human rights education, a study of 19 countries: Normative development.* San Jose, CA: IIDH.

Kati, K., & Gjedia, R. (2003). *Educating the next generation: Incorporation human rights education in the public school system.* Minneapolis, MN: New Tactics in Human Rights Project.

Netherlands Helsinki Committee. (1995, October). *Human rights education: Planning for the future.* Soesterberg, the Netherlands: Netherlands Helsinki Committee.

Pearse, S. (1987). *European teachers' seminar on "human rights education in a global perspective."* Strasbourg, Austria: Council of Europe.

Ramirez, F. O., Suarez, D., & Meyer, J. W. (2007). The worldwide rise of human rights education. In A. Benavot & C. Braslavsky (Eds.), *School knowledge in comparative and historical perspective: Changing curricula in primary and secondary education* (pp. 35-52). Hong Kong: Comparative Education Research Centre and Springer.

Reardon, B. (1995). *Educating for human dignity.* Philadelphia: University of Pennsylvania Press.

South House Exchange. (2004). *Education for peace, human rights, democracy, international understanding and tolerance. Report of Canada.* Prepared for The Council of Ministers of Education, Canada in collaboration with the Canadian Commission for UNESCO.

Tibbitts, F. (1996). On human dignity: A renewed call for human rights education. *Social Education, 60*(7), 428-431.

Tibbitts, F. (2003, July 7-8). *Report from the United Nations Office of the High Commissioner sub-regional meeting on human rights education in Southeastern Europe.* Skopje, Macedonia: United Nations.

United Nations. (1996). *International plan of action for the decade of human rights education.* Geneva, Switzerland: United Nations.

United Nations. (1996). *Report of the United Nations High Commissioner for Human Rights on the implementation of the Plan of Action for the United Nations Decade for Human Rights.* Retrieved November 6, 2007, from http://www.unhchr.ch/huridocda/huridoca.nsf/(Symbol)/A.51.506.Add.1.En?OpenDocument

United Nations General Assembly. (2005). *Draft plan of action for the first phase (2005-2007) of the proposed World Programme for Human Rights Education* (A/59/525). New York: United Nations.

UNESCO. (1978). *Final document: International Congress on the Teaching of Human Rights*. SS-78/Conf.401/Col.29. Vienna, Austria.

UNESCO. (2005). *The plan for action for 2005-2009 in brief, the World Programme for Human Rights Education*. Retrieved November 6, 2007, from http://www.ohchr.org/english/issues/education/training/docs/PlanofActioninbrief_en.pdf

Yeban, F. (2003). Building a culture of human rights: Challenge to human rights education in 21st century. In *Human rights education pack* (pp. 28-31). Bangkok, Thailand: ARRC.

CHAPTER 13

GLOBAL CITIZENSHIP EDUCATION

Lynn Davies

INTRODUCTION: DEFINITIONS AND DEBATES

This article examines the nature of global citizenship education and how it could be part of peace education. This is a contested field, as definitions of "global citizenship" are not without problems. Also disputable is the question of what sort of education prepares someone to be a global citizen. We cannot be citizens of the world in the way that we are citizens of a nation (or, for an increasing minority of stateless people, would like to be). So, is global citizenship a fiction, a paradox? Does it have meaning for young people today?

While global education or world studies has been advocated and practiced in schools and colleges across the world since the 1970s, global citizenship education is a relatively new concept. The insertion of "citizenship" into global education implies something more than, or different from, previous conceptions. The linked question is whether global citizenship education is not simply more informed local citizenship education. In fact, global *citizenship* education is usually directly concerned with social justice rather than the more minimalist interpretations of

Encyclopedia of Peace Education, pp. 109–114
Copyright © 2008 by Information Age Publishing

global education that focus on "international awareness" or being a more well-rounded person. Neither is world citizenship education only about being economically active and technologically literate in a world system. Citizenship clearly has implications in terms of rights and responsibilities, duties and entitlements, concepts that are not necessarily explicit in global education. One can have emotions and multiple identities without doing much about them; citizenship implies an active role.

The U.K. Oxfam (1997) *A Curriculum for Global Citizenship* defined a "global citizen" as someone who:

- Is aware of the wider world and has a sense of their own role as a world citizen,
- respects and values diversity,
- has an understanding of how the world works economically, politically, socially, culturally, technologically and environmentally,
- is outraged by social injustice,
- is willing to act to make the world a more equitable and sustainable place,
- and participates in and contributes to the community at a range of levels from the local to the global. (p. 1)

In this definition, we see that empathy is not enough; there must be "outrage," so that motivations for change are high. This has profound implications for teaching and learning, and may not sit easily with current pedagogical philosophies tied to content knowledge and passing of examinations. The requirements for curriculum would be equally demanding in terms of the comprehensive understanding of how the world works and the preparation for active participation. This definition also raises the issue of whether a person in a low-income country who has little access to formal education or wide-ranging knowledge, and does not have the opportunity to participate internationally, can receive the title of a "global citizen." At one level, one could argue that we are all global citizens just by virtue of living in the world; yet clearly a global citizenship education, particularly one that facilitates peace, demands more than this.

A crucial but unresolved task concerns how people can "act to make the world a more equitable and sustainable place" (Oxfam, 1997, p. 3). For example, many people who felt paralyzed by the recent Iraq war participated in massive marches opposing the invasion, signed petitions, and wrote letters, and experienced the frustration of living in so-called democratic societies and being apparently unable to change the course of a government action that seemed fundamentally unjust. Nonetheless, the

OXFAM definition is important in drawing attention to the "active" role of global citizens.

Griffiths (1998) outlines the "shared agenda" that characterizes various international nongovernmental organizations, which suggests that global citizenship transcends the artificiality of national boundaries and regards "Planet Earth" as the common home of humanity. For him, the common identity which unites human beings is not primarily cultural, national, political, civil, social, or economic, but ethical. Global citizenship is based on rights, responsibility, and action.

> A picture, then, of the global citizen: not merely aware of her rights but able and desirous to act upon them; of an autonomous and inquiring critical disposition; but her decisions and actions tempered by an ethical concern for social justice and the dignity of humankind; therefore able, through her actions, to control and enhance the "trajectory of the self" through life while contributing to the commonweal, the public welfare, with a sense of civic duty to replenish society. (Griffiths, 1998, p. 40)

An important point is that for him, pupils should be accorded the rights of citizenship and educated not *in* or *about* citizenship, but *as* citizens. This implies a different ethos in the school from conventional practice, where teachers have more rights and responsibilities than students.

Osler and Starkey in various texts have argued that international human rights declarations, adopted by the whole international community, provide a common set of universal values that can be used to make judgments about global issues and about implied responsibilities to respect the rights of others (see for example Osler & Starkey 2000). It seems that the growing acceptance of, or publicity given to, international rights conventions have impacted on the discourse surrounding global citizenship. It must be acknowledged, however, that although international rights conventions are intended to "guarantee" rights, they are still enacted primarily at the national or local levels. Legal knowledge in global citizenship education is also needed, in order to be aware of how international conventions are translated into various national acts and where gaps or loopholes might be found.

One of the important tensions in global citizenship, then, is how to treat "culture." In discussions of cultural integration, there is often the language of "one's own culture" and "others' culture," yet this notion of "us" and "them" becomes more complex in a world of migration and dual or hybrid identities. Under a human rights framework, respect for "others" is problematized when cultural practices infringe upon the rights of some members of society, at which point there must at least be a debate. Osler (2000) noted that while cultural pluralism propounds openness to all cultures,

> that openness [does] not mean accepting any position proffered but ... instead being willing to give a genuine hearing to the reasons for any position held. The respect that cultural pluralism calls for is critical respect. The critique must be carried out in practice. The outcome cannot be guaranteed. (p. 56)

So, together with outrage, we have another possibly uncomfortable prospect for teachers in any country with a national curriculum and assessment guidelines: an outcome of a critical debate that is not guaranteed.

Culture is not simply about origins but also concerns current linkages, international trade, and economies. Some argue that we are all becoming global citizens whether we like it or not: the spread of international conventions gives us common rights and entitlements, but on the other hand, the globalization of trade and concentration of economic power may erode some of these rights. Globalization can be seen as both a threat and an opportunity in terms of the varied impacts of trade, technology, media, social organization, and cultures. For Brownlie (2001),

> Global citizenship is more than learning about seemingly complex "global issues" such as sustainable development, conflict and international trade— important as these are. It is also about the global dimension to local issues, which are present in all out lives, localities, and communities. (p. 2)

The now familiar slogan, "act locally, think globally," is an attempt to overcome some of the problems in what can be an abstracted or far-removed concept of global citizenship. Because of the mesh of international linkages, the idea is that a local action (for example regarding pollution or choices that contribute to global warming) could have a wider impact.

THE LINK WITH PEACE EDUCATION

The concept of "multiple identities" contains the idea that we have a number of cultural facets to our personal identities and, more importantly, loyalties. Yet this now taken-for-granted concept is in danger of lacking meaning in practice. Are multiple identities something that people "naturally" have, that they acquire, or that they try to have? It is significant that only one or two people are needed to fan the fires of hostility and begin a conflict, but in order to achieve peace and security, very broad and strong bandings of people are needed who are comfortable with notions of multiple identities, and who have enough in common to work together. These groups will have found ways to work with diversity.

A global citizenship identity contains first, the recognition that conflict and peace are rarely confined to national boundaries, and second, that even stable societies are implicated in wars elsewhere, whether by default (choosing not to intervene) or actively in terms of aggression and invasion. A third or middle dimension to the usual phrase needs to be added: "act locally, analyze nationally, and think globally." Migration, for example, is a global phenomenon; but national policies on immigrants, refugees, and asylum seekers have highly local implications. How robust is our acceptance of "multiple identities" and "dynamic cultures?" How far are we prepared to take action to defend the rights of those whom others see as threatening the local culture and economy? Who counts as a citizen in our own backyard or local school? These questions might be the true tests of a vibrant global citizenship education.

In a study examining the needs of teachers and learners in global citizenship education in the United Kingdom (Davies, Harber, & Yamashita, 2004), the predominant issue that young people were interested in was war. This was not war in any historical context, but rather current conflicts (specifically, at that time, the Iraq conflict). Students wanted to understand the causes of war, the reasons for hatred, and the reasons for U.K. involvement. They felt that many of their teachers avoided the topic for fear of raising ethnic tensions in their multicultural classrooms. But young people were aware that they might receive biased or superficial views from the media, and felt it was the school's role to provide deeper understandings of conflict.

Another key point that emerged from this study concerned the school's attitude towards activism. The logic of active citizenship education suggests that schools should encourage young people to take political action where they saw a need or when they were outraged by an injustice, as discussed earlier. Yet many schools are wary of such involvement. In the U.K., students in some schools who took time off to join marches against the Iraq war were punished or labeled as truants. The key task of any citizenship education should be to give students a disposition to participate in politics—not only by voting but through actions to improve local or global communities.

Thus, a global citizenship education for peace would be a highly political education, not simply a bland multiculturalism, unquestioning "tolerance" or "being nice to each other." It has four interrelated components: knowledge, analysis, skills, and action (KASA). First, there is the knowledge of world current events, economics, and international relations. Second is the capacity to critically analyze media, religious messages, dogma, superstition, hate literature, extremism, and fundamentalism. Third, it involves political skills, such as persuasion, negotiation, lobbying, campaigning, and demonstrating. Fourth are dispositions for joint action, which these days include networking through communications technology, starting a Web site, or joining international forums of young people working for peace. These are all essential ingredients for a solid global citizenship education for peace that can produce active world citizens who understand the causes and effects of conflict, who do not join radical groups, who vote out politicians who go to war, who do not support religious leaders who preach hate, and who join others to make their voice for peace more potent.

REFERENCES

Brownlie, A. (2001). *Citizenship education: The global dimension, guidance for key stages 3 and 4*. London: Development Education Association.

Davies, L., Harber, C., & Yamashita, L. (2004). *The needs of teachers and learners in global citizenship* (Report of DFID funded project). Birmingham, England: Centre for International Education and Research.

Griffiths, R. (1998). *Educational citizenship and independent learning*. London: Jessica Kingsley.

Osler, A. (2000). *Citizenship and democracy in schools: Diversity, identity, equality*. Stoke on Trent, England: Trentham.

Osler, A., & Starkey, H. (2000). Citizenship, human rights and cultural diversity. In *Citizenship and democracy in schools: Diversity, identity, equality*. Stoke, England: Trentham.

Oxfam. (1997). *A curriculum for global citizenship*. Oxford, England: Oxfam.

SECTION IV

Frameworks and
New Directions for Peace Education

The chapters thus far have provided information about where peace education has come from, key ideas that have shaped where it is now, and what shared understandings unify scholars and practitioners in the field. This section explores disciplinary frameworks and forward-looking ideas for the field in an attempt to engage in dialogue about the way ahead. Societies are increasingly connected, yet also increasingly unequal, and peace education may have a role to play providing research and practice that can address manifestations of direct and structural violence. This section addresses suggestions for scholars and practitioners based on developments in the field to date and preferred visions for the future.

QUESTIONS TO CONSIDER

- School is but one place where youth are socialized into the norms of any society. What are the strengths and limitations of school-based peace education, and in what other arenas can peace education be developed?

Encyclopedia of Peace Education, pp. 115–116
Copyright © 2008 by Information Age Publishing
All rights of reproduction in any form reserved.

- Considerable attention has been focused on discussing the future in various chapters of this volume. How does a "futures" perspective inform the form, content, and pedagogy of peace education?
- How does the need for "unity" in postconflict settings interact with the need for justice for human rights abuses? To what extent are the two perspectives compatible? How can justice and peace coexist in a way that enhances both?

CHAPTER 14

COMPARATIVE AND INTERNATIONAL EDUCATION AND PEACE EDUCATION

Robin J. Burns

INTRODUCTION

Comparative and international education constitutes two linked fields of educational research and theorizing. While the distinction is not a rigid one, comparative education includes the more "academic, analytic, and scientific aspects of the field", while international education "is related to cooperation, understanding, and exchange elements" (Rust, 2002, p. iii).

Comparative Education

The field has not been rigidly defined. However, implicit in the notion of "comparative" is the study of more than one unit, and since comparative education arose at a time when national systems of education were being formed, the nation-state has been the primary unit of study. An early comparative education scholar, I. L. Kandel (1933), suggested that "The problems and purposes of education have in general become

Encyclopedia of Peace Education, pp. 117–125
Copyright © 2008 by Information Age Publishing
All rights of reproduction in any form reserved.

somewhat similar in most countries; the solutions are influenced by differences of tradition, and culture peculiar to each" so that the task of a comparative scholar is to "discuss the meaning of general education, elementary and secondary, in the light of the forces—political, social, and cultural—which determine the character of national systems of education" (p. xi). The field now includes all levels of education, formal and nonformal. Kandel did not specify the role of actual comparison of systems, the nature and purpose of which has not only proved controversial methodologically (Rust, 2001), but has in recent decades also been criticized on the grounds of resulting in inappropriate educational transfers especially from "center" to "periphery" nations (Ball, 1998; Crossley & Jarvis, 2001; Jones, 1998; Tikly, 2001; Zachariah, 1979). Multisystem studies constitute less than 33% of the reported research within comparative education journals (Rust, Soumaré, Pescador, & Shibuya, 1999). Though still controversial, intrasystem comparisons are also undertaken (Crossley & Jarvis, 2000; Kelly & Altbach, 1986; Ross, 2002; Welch, 1991; Welch & Masemann, 1997).

International Education

Internationalism is an underlying motif in the formation and development of comparative studies in education. Altbach and Kelly (1986) note that:

> The improvement of international understanding in general and education in particular is a long-standing tradition in the field. There has always been and, we hope, will continue to be a humanitarian and ameliorative element that has impelled many comparative educators to become involved in international programs to improve aspects of education and to encourage increased international understanding, particularly in the schools, as a contribution to world peace and development. (p. 4)

The "ameliorative" element, which forms the basis on which peace education comes within the domain of comparative education, is found mostly in the alliance between academic educational researchers and educational policymakers and planners. This aspect has been present in the field since the 1820s when the founding father, Jullien de Paris, was concerned with the induction of principles of policy from the collection, classification and analysis of foreign data (Holmes, 1985). Comparative educators have been involved subsequently in two international data collection agencies since their inception: the International Bureau of Education and United Nations Educational, Scientific, and Cultural Organization (UNESCO). With the inclusion of education in the economic development formulae of modernization theories in the 1960s and 1970s, the comparative tools for comparing educational outcomes cross-nationally were sought by agencies seeking "human capital" development outcomes.

Whether or not such "applied" research is "international" rather than "comparative" has been controversial (Wilson, 1994). International includes the study of international educational institutions and incorporates concerns by educators with "the development of multicultural and global efficacy" for a just society (Arnove, 2001, p. 501). Certainly comparativists operate transnationally as researchers and in their professional associations, especially the World Council of Comparative Education Societies (WCCES) and regional comparative education associations.

Debates continue on the extent of the field, appropriate subject-matter, and methodology. They are highlighted in presidential addresses to national societies and in the editorials of the major journals. Altbach's (1991) depiction of a "multidisciplinary field that looks at education ... in a cross-cultural context" (p. 491) broadly summarizes the situation.

A CHANGING FIELD

The debate about comparative *and* international education indicates the development of the field of study and the changes over time that have facilitated or inhibited the inclusion of peace education as a legitimate topic for study. Three major periods in the recent development of comparative and international education can be distinguished. The first, from the early post-World War II years to the 1970s, was characterized by concern with methodology and with applying an analytical, inductive scientific approach to the study of educational systems. In the second, from the late 1970s onwards critiques of positivism and structural-functional theorizing began to affect the social sciences and humanities, the base disciplines for many comparativists. Alternative methodologies such as hermeneutics and critical theory came to the fore in comparative education, and with them, a critique of the state as the principal unit of analysis (e.g., Altbach, 1991; Kelly & Altbach, 1986; Crossley & Broadfoot, 1992; Open File, 1989; Welch, 1985; Welch, 1992; Welch & Burns, 1992). This debate continues today (Cook, Hite, & Epstein, 2004; Cowen, 1996; Dale & Robertson, 2005; Marginson & Mollis, 2001; Rust et al., 1999; Schriewer, 2006; Tikly & Crossley, 2001; Torres, 2001).

Exploration of the educational implications of globalization serves as an umbrella for comparative and international education in its third and current phase (in addition to works in the previous paragraph, see

Arnove, 2001; Carnoy & Rhoten, 2002a, 2002b; Crossley & Jarvis, 2000; Crossley & Jarvis, 2001; Crossley, & Watson, 2003; Dale & Robertson, 2005; Mehta & Ninnes, 2003). This phase is characterized by increasing diversification of theories, subjects, methodologies, and methods as comparativists address the question: "what is the comparative advantage of comparative education in understanding the changing social context of education and some of the secular dilemmas of equity, equality, and quality of education throughout the world?" (Torres, 2001, p. viii). Studies of educational planning, development and reform, ethnicity, race and class, and gender and sexual orientation showed the greatest increase in published comparative and international educational research between 1997-2004 (Raby, 2005).

Today, comparative and international education is a complex field characterized by multiple methodological approaches and topics of study. The ameliorative element has been applied to the "improvement" of educational planning and systems. More recently, critique of the focus on the nation-state, and of the ways in which educational knowledge reinforces existing power and status structures within and between societies, and the acknowledgment of the impact of globalization on equity and justice, has opened new topics for research and teaching. International understanding, cooperation, human rights, peace, and related issues such as the environment are considered, if at all, as issues for teaching within comparative education.

PEACE EDUCATION WITHIN COMPARATIVE AND INTERNATIONAL EDUCATION

Reflections on the origins of comparative and international education, especially in the post-World War II period, suggest that one thread is the response by educators to the realities and consequences of war. Peace education does not have a strong position in academic educational institutions and there has been only one chair of peace education, held by Lennart Vriens at the University of Utrecht, the Netherlands. It is barely visible in comparative and international education, at least in the international journals in the field, *Comparative Education, Compare, Comparative Education Review, Canadian and International Education,* and the *International Review of Education (IRE).* The first two are edited in the United Kingdom, the third in the United States, the fourth in Canada and the last by the UNESCO Institute at Hamburg.

Given the work undertaken by UNESCO within the framework of its *Recommendation Concerning Education for International Understanding, Cooperation and Peace and Education Relating to Human Rights and Fundamental*

Freedoms, adopted by the general conference in 1974, it is not surprising that most of the articles on peace or related education published in comparative and international journals are found in the *IRE*, including a special edition in 1983 edited by Norwegians Magnus Haavelsrud and Johan Galtung, neither a comparative educator. All the contributors were members of the Peace Education Commission (PEC) of the International Peace Research Association and one means for a comparative perspective on peace education is the existence of PEC and its *Journal of Peace Education*, launched in 2004.

Writers frequently link "international understanding" with "peace," as in the 1979 special, 25th anniversary edition of the *IRE*: "It is increasingly important to take international action for the avoidance of war and for the safeguarding of the human environment" (Elvin, 1979, p. 461; see also Brock-Utne, 1988; Vriens, 1990). The issues of global security (Williams, 2000), culture and diversity (Simkin, 1998), and class (Welch, 1993) have been taken up by some comparative and international educators and are relevant to the debate about the formation and transmission of a "culture of peace," which is essentially internationalist (see e.g., Adams, 2000; Page, 2004; Vriens, 1993; for a relational approach which can have an international dimension, Ross, 2002). Bjerstedt (1993), Brock-Utne (1988, 2000), Burns and Aspeslagh (1996a and 1996b), Halperin (1997), Heater (1984), Iram (2003), Ray (1988) and Reardon (1987, 1988) are among the peace educators who point out the complex relationships between peace education, education for international understanding, and related fields such as human rights education. Harber (1997) and Davies (2005), both writing in *Compare*, and Zajda, Majhanovich, & Rust (2006) turn the issues on their head by problematizing education itself as a potential source of conflict as well as for social justice.

However, articles on peace education, education for human rights and civic education appear only rarely even in the *IRE*. Nothing has appeared on peace education in *Comparative Education* or the *Comparative Education Review*, though there have been articles on civic education, internationalized education, moral education, political education, political socialization, education for democracy, and human rights education. *Compare* has had several relevant articles in the past 25 years, most recently the British Association for International and Comparative Education 2004 presidential address (Davies, 2005). Since 1996, within the comparative education societies, "peace and justice" is one stream in the WCCES congresses, and the Comparative and International Education Society now has a peace education special interest group, some of whose members have published monographs on the subject, but have not yet published in the comparative education journals.

Burns and Aspeslagh (1996b) consider that comparative education provides "a way to understand the development of educational ideas and their practice, in concrete settings" (p. 9), arguing that this is an appropriate way to study peace education. However, peace educators are still largely concerned with issues such as children's attitudes, descriptions of particular peace education initiatives, and polemics related to the introduction of peace education in formal education systems. While the latter is clearly suitable for comparative research, the ongoing preoccupation of comparative education with systems of education and the fact that peace education rarely becomes incorporated as such within a system is another factor keeping the fields apart.

CONCLUSION

New developments in comparative and international education, especially critiques of globalization and its impact on education, employment, human relations and culture, presage new possibilities to bring the fields closer. A clear challenge is found in Davies (2005) contention that

> the relationship between education and conflict includes the more obvious effect of war and violence on education itself ... but there is the perhaps less obvious reverse impact of education on conflict ... through the reproduction or amplification of inequality, exclusion and social polarization; through the hardening of ethnic or religious identifications and divisions; and through its acceptance of dominant macho, aggressive, militaristic, and homophobic masculinities. (p. 359)

REFERENCES

Adams, D. (2000). From the international year to a decade for a culture of peace and non-violence. *International Journal of Curriculum and Instruction Special Issue, 2*(1), 1-10.
Altbach, P. G. (1991). Trends in comparative education. *Comparative Education Review, 35*(3), 491-507.
Altbach, P. G., & Kelly, G. P. (1986). Introduction: Perspectives on comparative education. In P. G. Altbach & G. P. Kelly (Eds.), *New approaches to comparative education* (pp. 1-10). Chicago: The University of Chicago Press.
Arnove, R. F. (2001). Comparative and international education society (CIES) facing the twenty-first century: Challenges and contributions. *Comparative Education Review, 45*(4), 477-503.
Ball, S. J. (1998). Big policies/small world: An introduction to international perspectives in education policy. *Comparative Education, 34*(2), 119-130.

Bjerstedt, Å. (Ed.). (1993). *Peace education: Global perspectives.* Stockholm, Sweden: Almqvist & Wiksell.

Brock-Utne, B. (1988). Formal education as a force in shaping cultural norms relating to war and the environment. In A. Westing (Ed.). *Cultural norms, war, and the environment* (pp. 83-100). Oxford, England: Oxford University Press.

Brock-Utne, B. (2000). Peace education in era of globalization. *Peace Review, 12*(1), 131-138.

Burns, R. J., & Aspeslagh, R. (Eds). (1996a) *Three decades of peace education around the world. An anthology.* New York: Garland.

Burns, R. J., & Aspeslagh, R. (1996b). Peace education and the comparative study of education. In *Three decades of peace education around the world. An anthology* (pp. 3-23). New York: Garland.

Carnoy, M., & Rhoten. D. (Eds). (2002a). The meanings of globalization for education change. *Comparative Education Review Special Issue, 46*(1), 1-154.

Carnoy, M., & Rhoten. D. (2002b) What does globalization mean for education change? A comparative approach. *Comparative Education Review, 46*(1), 1-9.

Cook, B. J., Hite, S. J., & Epstein, E. H. (2004). Discerning trends, contours, and boundaries in comparative education: A survey of comparativists and their literature. *Comparative Education Review, 48*(2), 123-150.

Cowen, R. (Ed.). (1996). Last past the post: Comparative education, modernity, and perhaps post-modernity. *Comparative Education Special Number (18), 32*(2), 151-170.

Crossley, M., & Broadfoot, P. (1992). Comparative and international research in education: Scope, problems and potential. *British Educational Research Journal, 18*(2), 99-112.

Crossley, M., & Jarvis, P. (Eds). (2000). Comparative education for the twenty-first century: An international response. *Comparative Education Special Number (23), 36*(3).

Crossley, M., & Jarvis, P. (Eds). (2001). Comparative education for the twenty-first century: An international response. *Comparative Education Special Number (24), 37*(4)

Crossley M., & Watson, K. (2003). *Comparative and international research in education: Globalization, context and difference.* London/New York: Routledge Falmer.

Dale, R., & Robertson, S.L. (Eds). (2005) Globalisation and education in knowledge economies and knowledge societies. *Comparative Education Special Issue (30), 41*(2), 117-242.

Davies, L. (2005). Schools and war: Urgent agendas for comparative and international education. *Compare, 35*(4), 357-371.

Elvin, L. (1979). International understanding. *International Review of Education, 25*, 461-476.

Halperin, D. S. (Ed.). (1997). *To live together: Shaping new attitudes to peace through education.* Paris, France: UNESCO International Bureau of Education.

Harber, C. (1997). International developments and the rise of education for democracy. *Compare, 27*(2), 179-191.

Heater, D. B. (1984). *Peace through education: The contribution of the Council for Education in World Citizenship.* London: Falmer Press.

Holmes, B. (1985). Trends in comparative education. *Prospects, 15*(3), 325-346.

Iram, Y. (Ed.). (2003). *Education of minorities and peace education in pluralistic societies*. Westport, CT: Praeger.

Jones, P. W. (1998). Globalisation and internationalism: Democratic prospects for world education. *Comparative Education, 34*(2), 143-156.

Kandel, I. L. (1933). *Studies in comparative education*. Londony: George Harrap.

Kelly, G. P., & Altbach, P. G. (1986). Comparative education: Challenge and response. *Comparative Education Review, 30*(1), 89-107.

Marginson, S., & Mollis, M. (2001). "The door opens and the tiger leaps": Theories and reflexivities of comparative education for a global millennium. *Comparative Education Review, 45*(4), 581-615.

Mehta, S., & Ninnes, P. (2003). Postmodernism debates and comparative education: a critical discourse analysis. *Comparative Education Review, 47*(2), 238-257.

Open File. (1989). Comparative education: A provisional stocktaking. *Prospects, 19*(3), 351-406.

Page, J. (2004). Peace education: Exploring some philosophical foundations. *International Review of Education, 50*(1), 3-15.

Raby, R. L. (2005). Reflections on the field: A review of the 2004 *Comparative Education Review* bibliography. *Comparative Education Review, 49*(3), 410-418.

Ray, D. (Ed.). (1988). *Peace education: Canadian and international perspectives*. London: Third Eye.

Reardon, B. A. (1987). *From international understanding to peace education and world order studies* (Reprints and Miniprints No. 579). Sweden: Department of Education and Psychological Research, Malmö School of Education, University of Lund.

Reardon, B. A. (1988). *Comprehensive peace education: educating for global responsibility*. New York: Teachers College Press.

Ross, H. (2002). The space between us: The relevance of relational theories to comparative and international education. *Comparative Education Review, 46*(4), 407-433.

Rust, V. (2001). Editorial. *Comparative Education Review, 45*(3), iii-iv.

Rust, V. (2002). The place of international education in the Comparative Education Review. *Comparative Education Review, 46*(3), iii-iv.

Rust, V., Soumaré, A., Pescador, O., & Shibuya, M. (1999). Research strategies in comparative education. *Comparative Education Review, 43*(1), 86-109.

Schriewer, J. (Ed.). (2006). Comparative methodologies in the social sciences— cross-disciplinary inspirations. *Comparative Education Special Issue, 42*(32).

Simkin, K. (1998, December 6-9). *Education for intercultural understanding: Some implications for comparative education*. Paper presented at the 26th annual conference of the Australia and New Zealand Comparative and International Education Society, Auckland, New Zealand: University of Auckland.

Tikly, L. (2001). Globalisation and education in the post colonial world: Towards a conceptual framework. *Comparative Education, 37*(2), 151-172.

Tikly, L., & Crossley, M. (2001). Teaching comparative and international education: A framework for analysis. *Comparative Education Review, 45*(4), 561-580.

Torres, C. A. (2001). Globalization and comparative education in the world system. *Comparative Education Review, 45*(4), iii-x.

Vriens, L. (1990). *Peace education in the nineties: A reappraisal of values and options* (Peace Education Miniprints No. 4). Lund University, Sweden: Malmo School of Education.

Vriens, L. (1993, August 10-14). *Nationalism, democracy and education: The alternative of internationalism.* Paper presented to the 12th International Human Science Research Conference, Groningen, The Netherlands.

Welch, A. R. (1985). The functionalist tradition in comparative education. *Comparative Education, 21*(1), 5-19.

Welch, A. R. (1991). Knowledge and legitimation in comparative education. *Comparative Education Review, 35*(3), 508-531.

Welch, A. R. (1992). Knowledge, culture and power: Educational knowledge and legitimation in comparative education. In R. J. Burns & A. R. Welch (Eds.), *Contemporary perspectives in comparative education* (pp. 35-68). New York: Garland.

Welch, A. R. (1993). Class, culture and the state in comparative education: Problems, perspectives and prospects. *Comparative Education, 29*(1), 7-27.

Welch, A. R., & Burns, R. J. (Eds). (1992). *Contemporary perspectives in comparative education.* New York: Garland.

Welch, A., & Masemann, V. (1997). Editorial introduction. *International Review of Education, 43*(5-6), 393-399.

Williams, C. (2000). Education and human survival: The relevance of the global security framework to international education. *International Review of Education, 46*(3-4), 183-203.

Wilson, D. N. (1994). Comparative and international education: Fraternal or Siamese twins? A preliminary genealogy of our twin fields. *Comparative Education Review, 38*(4), 449-486.

Zachariah, M. (1979). Comparative educators and international development policy. *Comparative Education Review, 23*(3), 341-354.

Zajda, J., Majhanovich, S., & Rust, V. (Eds). (2006). *Education and social justice.* Dordrecht: Springer.

CHAPTER 15

FUTURES EDUCATION

David Hicks

INTRODUCTION

While peace education is concerned with a wide variety of issues that manifest at scales from the local to the global, such issues cannot be understood without an exploration of the interrelationships between past, present, and future. While history deals with the past and most of education deals with the present, explicit exploration of the future is still often a missing dimension in education.

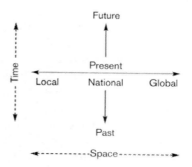

Figure 15.1. The spatial and temporal dimensions.

Internationally, educators use the term "futures education" or "futures in education" to refer to this concern. However, it is more useful to talk of the need for a "futures dimension" in the curriculum and for people to be able to take a "futures perspective" on their lives and society more widely. Put at its simplest, this refers to a form of education which *promotes the knowledge, understanding and skills that are needed in order to think more*

Encyclopedia of Peace Education, pp. 127–133
Copyright © 2008 by Information Age Publishing
All rights of reproduction in any form reserved.

critically and creatively about the future. Clearly, peace education needs to contain such a dimension and promote such a perspective since two of the key questions it explores in relation to self and society are "Where do we want to get to?" and "How do we get there?" (Hicks, 2004)

FUTURES STUDIES

While interest in the future is as old as humanity itself, serious investigation in futures really only emerged after World War II in the form of strategic planning, technological forecasting, economic analysis, and the establishment of the first major think tanks. While much of this endeavor focused on economic and military forecasting, there were other, largely European, initiatives which were more concerned with how such thinking could be used to help create better social futures (Masini, 2006).

Futures studies as a field of academic inquiry emerged in the 1960s. It is a broad field of concern, and Inayatullah (1993) notes that it "largely straddles two dominant modes of knowledge—the technical concerned with predicting the future and the humanist concerned with developing a good society" (p. 236). It is the latter strand which underpins the work of the World Futures Studies Federation (WFSF) (www.wfsf.org) set up in 1972. One of the founders of WFSF was Johan Galtung, then Director of the International Peace Research Institute in Oslo.

Bell (1997) argues that the purpose of futures studies is to "discover or invent, examine, evaluate and propose possible, probable and preferable futures" (p. 73). He continues, "futurists seek to know: what can or could be (the possible), what is likely to be (the probable), and what ought to be (the preferable)" (p. 73). Dator (2005) elaborates further:

> The future cannot be studied because the future does not exist. Futures studies does not ... pretend to study the future. It studies ideas about the future... (which) often serve as the basis for actions in the present.... Different groups often have very different images of the future. Men's images may differ from women's. Western images may differ from non-Western, and so on. (para. 8)

One of the main tasks of futures studies is to identify and examine the major alternative futures which exist at any given time and place. The future cannot be predicted, but preferred futures can and should be envisioned, invented, implemented, continuously evaluated, revised, and reenvisioned. Thus, another major task of futures studies is to facilitate individuals and groups in formulating, implementing, and reenvisioning their preferred futures.

Elsewhere, Dator (2002, p. 10) argues that despite the variety of people's views of the future, all the images he has encountered, in whatever culture, can be grouped into four broad categories: *continuation* —a "business as usual" scenario, generally based on notions of continuing economic growth; *collapse*—a "catastrophe" scenario arising, for example, from economic instability, environmental disaster, terrorist attack; *disciplined society*—based on some set of overarching values, for example, traditional, ecological, God-given; and *transformational society*—a break from current norms based on "high-tech" or "high spirit" values.

Futures studies should not be seen as an internally-consistent endeavor. While key texts such as *Knowledge Base of Futures Studies* (Slaughter, 2005), *Advancing Futures* (Dator, 2002) and *Foundations of Futures Studies* (Bell, 1997) illustrate the breadth of concern, there are also major ideological debates within the field. Most notably, this has involved critiques of futures studies as being largely a White Western endeavor (Inayatullah, 1998; Sardar, 1999; Kapoor, 2001) and a primarily masculine discourse (Milojevic, 2004).

FUTURES IN EDUCATION

In varying degrees, educators have drawn on the academic field of futures studies in order to enrich their work in elementary and secondary school, and in teacher education. It can be argued that nine key concepts underlie the notion of a futures dimension.

1. State of the world
    In the early twenty-first century, the state of the world continues to give cause for concern. Issues dealing with sustainability, gaps between wealth and poverty, peace and conflict, and violations of human rights all have a major impact both locally and globally. We need to know about the causes of such problems, how they will affect our lives now and in the future, and the action needed to help resolve them.

2. Managing change
    In periods of rapid social and technological change, the past cannot provide an accurate guide to the future. Anticipation and adaptability, foresight and flexibility, innovation and intuition, become increasingly essential tools for survival. We need to develop such skills in order to become more adaptable and proactive towards change.

3.   Views of the future
     People's views of the future may vary greatly depending, for
     example, on age, gender, class and culture, as well as their
     attitudes to change, the environment and technology. We need
     to be aware of how views of the future thus differ and the ways in
     which this affects people's priorities in the present.

4.   Alternative futures
     At any point in time, a range of different futures is possible. It is
     useful to distinguish between probable futures, that is, those
     which seem *likely* to come about, and preferable futures, that is,
     those one feels *should* come about. We need to explore a range
     of probable and preferable futures, from the personal and local
     to the global.

5.   Hopes and fears
     Hopes and fears for the future often influence decision making
     in the present. Fears can lead to the avoidance of problems
     rather than their resolution. Clarifying hopes for the future can
     enhance motivation in the present and thus positive action for
     change. We need to explore our own hopes and fears for the
     future and learn to work creatively with them.

6.   Past/present/future
     Interdependence exists across both space and time. Past,
     present and future are inextricably connected. We are directly
     linked back in time by the oldest members of the community
     and forward into the next century by those born today. We need
     to explore these links and to gain a sense of both continuity and
     change as well as of responsibility for the future.

7.   Visions for the future
     The first decade of the new century provides a valuable
     opportunity for reviewing the state of society. What needs to be
     left behind and what taken forward? In particular, what visions
     of a better future are needed to motivate active and responsible
     citizenship in the present? We therefore need to develop our
     skills of envisioning and use of the creative imagination.

8.   Future generations
     Economists, philosophers, and international lawyers
     increasingly recognize the rights of future generations. It has
     been suggested that no generation should inherit less human

and natural wealth than the one that preceded it. We need to discuss the rights of future generations and what the responsibility to uphold these may involve.

9. Sustainable futures
    Current consumerist lifestyles on this planet are increasingly seen as unsustainable often causing more damage than benefit. A sustainable society would prioritize concern for the environment, the poorest members of the community, and the needs of future generations. We need to understand how this applies to our everyday lives and possible future employment.

One of the first writers to draw attention to the need for a futures dimension in the curriculum was Toffler (1974) in his still very relevant *Learning for Tomorrow: The Role of the Future in Education*. His key thesis remains as true now as then:

> All education springs from images of the future and all education creates images of the future. Thus all education, whether so intended or not, is a preparation for the future. Unless we understand the future for which we are preparing, we may do tragic damage to those we teach. (1974, cover)

It is interesting that Toffler wrote these words in the decade that saw the rise of neoconservative and neo-liberal ideologies which dominate so much of education today (Apple, 2006).

During the 1990s, there has been a growing interest in research on young people's images of the future and the implications of these images on education (Hicks & Holden, 1995). Hutchinson (1996) has carried out exciting work in the field of secondary education (including the influences on young people's views of the future) as has Page (2000) in relation to the early childhood curriculum, and Gidley and Inayatullah (2002) in relation to youth futures. A range of case studies of futures in education, from primary to tertiary level, are to be found in Hicks and Slaughter (1998), and a variety of classroom activities can be found in Pike and Selby (1999), Hicks (2001, 2006) and Slaughter and Bussey (2006), While Gidley et al. (2002) have explored recent developments in Australia.

ENVISIONING THE FUTURE

A number of interesting studies have explored the nature of young people's probable and preferable futures. Eckersley (1999) reported that

Australian youth were particularly concerned about pollution and environmental destruction, the gulf between rich and poor, high unemployment, conflict, crime and alienation, discrimination and prejudice, and economic difficulties. Eight out of 10 15-24 year-olds said that they would prefer a greener, more stable society, with an emphasis on cooperation, community and family, more equal distribution of wealth, and greater economic self-sufficiency. He concluded:

> Young people's preferred futures are undoubtedly idealized and utopian. Their significance lies in what they reveal about fundamental human needs ... and what they expect and what is being offered to them by world and national leaders. (p. 95)

This echoes much of the research that has been done on envisioning futures, albeit in Western contexts. It also echoes the findings of Elise Boulding (1988a, 1988b) from the numerous envisioning workshops that she ran in which she reported a preferred "baseline future" that often emerged. One should not, however, make the mistake of thinking that clear images of preferable futures are sufficient in themselves. As Meadows, Randers, and Meadows (2005) stress:

> We should say immediately, for the sake of sceptics, that we do not believe vision makes anything happen. Vision without action is useless. But action without vision is directionless and feeble. Vision is absolutely necessary to guide and motivate. More than that, vision when widely shared and firmly kept in sight, does bring into being new systems. (p. 272)

A futures perspective is crucial to effective teaching and learning in peace education. By enabling learners to think more critically and creatively about the forces that create probable and preferable futures, they are able to engage in more purposeful and focused action for change. This fulfils one of the tasks of the progressive educator which, Freire (1994) tells us, "is to unveil opportunities for hope, no matter what the obstacles might be" (p. 9).

REFERENCES

Apple, M. (2006). *Education the "right" way: Markets, standards, God, and inequality* (2nd ed.). London: Routledge Falmer.

Bell, W. (1997). *Foundations of futures studies*. New Brunswick, NJ: Transaction.

Boulding, E. (1988a). *Building a global civic culture*. New York: Teachers College Press.

Boulding, E. (1988b). Image and action in peace building. *Journal of Social Issues, 44*(2), 17-38.

Dator, J. (Ed.). (2002). *Advancing futures: Futures studies in higher education.* Westport, CT: Praeger.

Dator, J. (2005). Foreword. In R. Slaughter (Ed.), *Knowledge base of futures studies* [CD-ROM Professional Edition]. Retrieved November 6, 2007, from www.foresightinternational.com.au

Eckersley, R. (1999). Dreams and expectations: Young people's expected and preferred futures and their significance for education. *Futures, 31*, 73-90.

Freire, P. (1994). *A pedagogy of hope.* London: Continuum.

Gidley, J., & Inayatullah, S. (Eds.). (2002). *Youth futures: Comparative research and transformative visions.* Westport, CT: Praeger.

Hicks, D. (2001). *Citizenship for the future: A practical classroom guide.* Godalming, England: World Wide Fund for Nature UK.

Hicks, D. (2004). Teaching for tomorrow: how can futures studies contribute to peace education? *Journal of Peace Education, 1(1)*, 165-178.

Hicks, D. (2006). *Lessons for the future: The missing dimension in education.* Victoria, BC: Trafford.

Hicks, D., & Holden, C. (1995). *Visions of the future: Why we need to teach for tomorrow.* Stoke-on-Trent, England: Trentham Books.

Hicks, D., & Slaughter, R. (Eds.). (1998). *Futures education: The world yearbook of education 1998.* London: Kogan Page.

Hutchinson, F. (1996). *Educating beyond violent futures.* London: Routledge.

Inayatullah, S. (1993). From "who am I?" to "when am I?" Framing the shape and time of the future. *Futures, 25*, 235-253.

Inayatullah, S. (1998). Listening to non-Western perspectives, In D. Hicks & R. Slaughter, (Eds.), *Futures education: The world yearbook of education 1998* (pp. 55-68). London: Kogan Page.

Kapoor, R. (2001). Future as fantasy: forgetting the flaws. *Futures, 33*, 161-170.

Masini, E. (2006). Rethinking futures studies. *Futures, 38*, 1158-1168.

Meadows, D., Randers, J., & Meadows, D. (2005). *Limits to growth: The 30-year update.* London: Earthscan.

Milojevic, I. (2004). *Education futures: Dominating and contesting visions.* London: Routledge Falmer.

Page, J. (2000). *Reframing the early childhood curriculum: Educational imperatives for the future.* London: Routledge Falmer.

Pike, G., & Selby, D. (1999). *In the global classroom* (Vol. 1). Toronto, Canada: Pippin.

Sardar, Z. (1999). *Rescuing all our futures: The future of futures studies.* Westport, CT: Praeger.

Slaughter, R. (Ed.). (2005). *Knowledge base of futures studies* (Vols. 1-5). [CD-ROM Professional Edition]. Retrieved November 6, 2007, from www.foresightinternational.com.au

Slaughter, R., with Bussey, M. (2006). *Futures thinking for social foresight.* Taipei, Taiwan: Tamkang University Press. Retrieved November 6, 2007, from www.foresightinternational.com.au

Toffler, A. (1974). *Learning for tomorrow: The role of the future in education.* New York: Vintage Books.

CHAPTER 16

"CRITICAL"
PEACE EDUCATION

Monisha Bajaj

While "peace education" is a term often used for a variety of programs, studies, and initiatives, the field of peace education is one that includes a diverse array of scholarly perspectives, programmatic considerations, and underlying values. In this chapter, I argue for a reclaimed "critical peace education" in which attention is paid to issues of structural inequality and research aimed towards local understandings of how participants can cultivate a sense of transformative agency assumes a central role. Attention to research and the renewed pursuit of critical structural analyses (Galtung, 1969) can further the field towards scholar-activism in pursuit of peace education's emancipatory promise. For the purpose of this chapter, I define the goal of peace education, based on scholarly developments to date, as the transformation of educational content, structure, and pedagogy to address direct and structural forms of violence at all levels (Harris, 2004; Reardon, 1988).

This chapter represents my reflections as a student, researcher, and scholar in the fields of human rights and peace education. I coordinate the concentration in peace education for graduate students studying international and comparative education at Teachers College, and advise

Encyclopedia of Peace Education, pp. 135–146
Copyright © 2008 by Information Age Publishing
All rights of reproduction in any form reserved.

dozens of the students who embark on graduate work in this field of study. The multiplicity of expectations, understandings, and meanings of peace education that students bring and take from the concentration has inspired this chapter which calls for renewed attention to and exploration of a "critical peace education" (Diaz-Soto, 2005; Mirra, 2008; Montgomery, 2006; Wulf, 1974).[1] Such an approach would offer greater scholarly rigor and increased emphasis on research in our evolving and interdisciplinary field of peace education.

The move towards greater empiricism in peace education echoes Salomon and Nevo's (2002) critique that there is confusion at the conceptual level as to what peace education is and this is exacerbated by a lack of scholarly research on the impact of peace education. The field would benefit from greater emphasis on both research for the sake of greater knowledge about local meanings and experiences, as well as research as a form of evaluation of peace education programs (Bajaj, 2004). In order to examine what I assert should constitute a reclaimed "critical peace education," it is important to delineate the types of peace education that exist and situate this approach accordingly.

APPROACHES TO RESEARCH AND PRACTICE IN PEACE EDUCATION

Haavelsrud (1996) identifies four types of disarmament education which can be, and have been, extended to the larger field of peace education to categorize the various orientations that exist within it (Burns & Aspelagh, 1983). The four categories are useful in understanding approaches to peace education in both research and practice.

The first category is the *idealistic approach* in which there are universal notions of problems and solutions and little attention is paid to distinct societal groups and their interactions. Haavelsrud (1996) cites the UNESCO (United Nations Educational, Scientific, and Cultural Organization) preamble as representative of this approach that asserts that wars begin "in the minds of men" and therefore the singular new generation, versus the "old," needs peace education to counter the violent tendencies throughout the world. The level of analysis is the individual and there is a focus on social cohesion. This approach, often espoused by nongovernmental organizations and international initiatives, ignores issues of structural inequalities in formulating peace education and, according to the author, may exclude action to promote peace.

The second approach is the *intellectual* one (Haavelsrud, 1996). The focus is on the academic study of peace and conflict issues to build knowledge among learners. Pluralistic views on peace/disarmament issues are represented so the educational content is generally accepted by different political actors. The intellectual approach needs both universal scientific content and political buy-in so that all actors are represented. The limitations of this approach, Haavelsrud argues, are that such supposed neutrality is fraught with contradictions and there is little mention of how understanding the situation can lead to reflection and strategies for action and change.

The *ideological* approach is the third approach (Haavelsrud, 1996). Rooted in a neo-Marxist analysis of schooling, the school is seen as an apparatus that reproduces social control by the dominant class (Althusser, 1979). As such, all curriculum (and hidden curriculum) will be partial to the interests of those in power because of the social and cultural reproduction that occurs in schools (Bourdieu & Passeron, 1977; Bowles & Gintis, 1976). Hence, peace education, it is argued, should occur outside of the formal educational system. From this perspective, schools as institutions embody violence (Harber, 2004) and therefore offer little towards promoting peace.

The fourth approach is the *politicization* approach (Haavelsrud, 1996). This approach acknowledges that education, along with other efforts towards social change outside of schools, has a constructive role to play in promoting peace. Anchoring schooling in its larger social context, Haavelsrud calls for a close link between research, education, and action in an overall process of social change. Educational form, content, and organizational structure should be aligned to promote peace education. Echoing Freire's (1970) emphasis on raising students' critical consciousness, this approach utilizes formal and non-formal education to inspire both reflection and action. This fourth category that calls for action around peace and justice issues, with attention to conceptions based on in-depth knowledge and investigation of local realities, is most akin to the reclaimed critical peace education that I argue is necessary for our field.

RECLAIMING A CRITICAL PEACE EDUCATION

The 1970s marked the turn towards a "critical peace education" advanced by scholars such as Wulf (1974). Rooted in the Frankfurt School of Social Research and arguing that conflict and social critique be essential elements, these scholars called for a focus on "the societal conditions of peace education" (Wulf, personal communication, 2007). Given the prior emphasis on direct forms of violence, this shift was important in addressing social and economic injustice as incompatible with comprehensive peace (Galtung, 1969). Specifically, Wulf (1974) notes:

[Critical peace education] stems from an explicit understanding of peace education as a criticism of society.... Central concepts of critical peace education [are] "structural violence," "organized peacelessness," and "participation," ... giv[ing] an impression of the interdependence of international and internal social structures of power and dependence in and outside school. (p. x)

While the focus shifted away from critical peace education towards a culture of peace and a postmodern approach in the 1990s (Wintersteiner, 1999), it seems appropriate to reclaim a "critical peace education" some 30 years after its elaboration given the usefulness of structural analyses in the current globalized context.

More recently, scholars have linked Paulo Freire's educational philosophy to peace education and titled it "critical peace education" (Diaz-Soto, 2005) without reference to Wulf's (1974) earlier work. In addressing wars that continue to be fought worldwide, Diaz-Soto grounds her call for a critical peace education in the United States based on a need to promote negative peace, or the absence of direct violence.[2] Her recommendations to educators are rooted in a Freirean analysis of power with the aim of consciousness raising: she further calls for "border crossing," "decolonization," "inclusion," "equitable economic distribution," and a reliance on "love as a paradigm" (Diaz-Soto, 2005, p. 96). Some of her analyses resonate with the ideas put forth in this chapter, particularly the call for attention to power, identity, and culture. However, absent in the parameters she sets forth is a call for greater research in the field which I assert is the way to tailor peace education research methods and practices to their local context. The prescriptive nature of literature in the field of peace education to date often fails to acknowledge the complex and diverse forms that peace education can and must take—guided by continued investigation in schools and communities globally—in order to effectively address its promise as a field of inquiry and grounded practice.

While the field's evolution reflects the conditions of the time, in the present age of globalized economic and political structures that are increasing disparities and simultaneously dismantling avenues for citizens to hold their governments accountable, it appears that renewed attention to larger structural realities, particularly in the global South and through engaged and systematic research, would prove beneficial in understanding the possibilities and limitations of peace education. Acknowledging the need for a critical approach to peace education that affirms diversity and a multiplicity of perspectives, it is important to outline the components of such an approach. While human rights principles often guide peace education research and initiatives, the debates about these universal principles in addition to the promise they hold for sustainable peace are integral to a renewed critical peace education approach.

LOCAL STRUGGLES FOR HUMAN RIGHTS AS A FRAMEWORK FOR A CRITICAL PEACE EDUCATION

While the concept of "human rights" has undergone considerable discussion and scrutiny, it has become a term for which a singular definition cannot be assumed. Scholars have critiqued the use of human rights discourse in U.S. foreign policy as a guise for the promotion of economic interests (Mirra, 2008) and as a form of "liberal imperialism" that policymakers selectively employ (Rieff, 1999). The contextualization of the moment in which the Universal Declaration of Human Rights (UDHR), the most influential, though not legally binding, human rights document is also important for critical peace education because of its analysis of power. Western notions of individual rights over collective rights, though being addressed by third generation human rights documents, reflected the limited perspectives of those included at the table in 1947. Only four of Africa's 54 nations were original signatories of the United Nations charter, and one of these four was the apartheid government of South Africa (United Nations, 2007).

Peace educators have advocated for the inclusion of human rights as a prescriptive framework for the advancement of positive peace (Reardon, 1997). Human rights, taken to mean those principles enshrined in the 30 articles of the UDHR and implemented as such, are de-linked from the larger conceptual debates, struggles, tensions, and contradictions discussed in other disciplines. By advocating the incorporation of one form of "human rights" (i.e., the normative framework developed by Western diplomats in 1947), peace educators risk losing out on valuable information provided by critiques that can better equip them to genuinely teach *for* and *about* human rights. Human rights are a natural framework for peace education, but treating them as static rather than dynamic, and sometimes contradictory, ignores their complexity.

One example of the tensions inherent in human rights is the issue of enforcement. Teaching students about issues of justice and international principles, particularly if they live in communities where such rights are not protected by the state, can create frustration and disillusionment rather than the transformative agency that peace educators seek to cultivate within students. A critical, yet optimistic, approach would introduce students to issues of asymmetrical power relations, structural violence, and how principles of human rights can inform action amidst such a context.

Critical peace education has an important role to play in situations where interethnic conflict is rife and where human rights abuses have occurred. The international trend towards peace education for victims of human rights abuses, such as the implementation of peace education curricula in refugee camps (Iner-Agency Network for Education in Emergencies, 2005), is a partial strategy since efforts must also be aimed at those who hold power in the respective contexts. Postconflict education often chants the mantra of "never again" with a silent "for our people" added on to the end of the phrase. Critical peace educators must engage in the serious reflective and historicized work of engaging individuals and communities in believing and acting towards "never again for *any* people" so that "victims" do not become "killers" as seen historically in many international contexts (Mamdani, 2002). As such, peace education must prioritize even-handedness in its treatment of perpetrators and victims of human rights violations as targets of peace education. Critical peace educators, rather than downloading a preset lesson plan from the internet, need local, historicized knowledge to inform strategies to revise textbooks, promote respect for differences through the media and popular culture, and engage in a comprehensive campaign for human rights and social justice.

Critical peace educators may do well to consider examining local practices and meaning-making around human rights—informed by local types of peace education—in order to better understand values and beliefs that can inform peace education from the bottom up. For example, Gandhian studies in India resonates profoundly with the tenets of peace education though not always recognized as such (Prasad, 1998). Such investigation of the local context echoes the participatory research that Freire implores educators to engage in so as to develop the generative themes that will enable dialogue and raise students' critical consciousness (Spener, 1990). By localizing human rights and abstaining from imposing universalistic notions, much information can be garnered about how greater justice can be achieved and what type of education can catalyze it.

Additionally, the teaching of human rights, with attention to local examples, would provide important historical references for concepts often considered foreign. Historians have noted the Western bias of the telling of the story of human rights, neglecting important struggles, such as the Haitian revolution (despite its shortcomings), which can inspire collective action towards greater equity and justice (Knight, 2005). There is much mutual learning that can take place if peace educators cast their gaze towards the local in order to understand the hybrid meanings created from economic, political, and cultural globalization. As human rights scholar Michael Ignatieff (2000) notes:

Human rights has gone global not because it serves the interests of the powerful but primarily because it has advanced the interests of the powerless. Human rights has gone global by going local, imbedding itself in the soil of cultures and world views independent of the West, in order to sustain ordinary people's struggles against unjust states and oppressive social practices. (p. 290)

Attention to local struggles legitimizes collective agency in pursuing justice through human rights. Nested within this larger human rights project is the issue of educational access and content as core principles. For critical peace educators, locally relevant curricula around human rights and justice issues must be developed with the aim of simultaneously cultivating participants' analyses of structural inequalities and a sense of agency in acting to address these issues.

AGENCY AS A CENTRAL FRAMEWORK

Educational studies began to examine student agency as a way of exploring diverse student responses to participation in unequal schools (Aronowitz & Giroux, 1993; Giroux, 1997; Willis, 1977). Located in the interstices of neo-Marxist and postmodern educational theories, studies of agency have largely identified two types of resistance—oppositional and transformative. Transformative agency, further conceptualized in critical pedagogy by scholars such as Giroux (1997), is rooted in Freire's notion of radical hope and illustrates "how moral and political agency come together to inspire both a discourse of hope and a political project that take seriously what it means to envision a better life and society" (Giroux, 1988, p. 38).

Education, according to Freire, must foster the critical consciousness of students that, coupled with opportunities for collective thinking and action, can catalyze transformative agency. Such a process, is instrumental to peace education efforts. Leading peace education scholar, Betty Reardon (2001), importantly mentions *global agency* as a core competency of peace education scholars and practitioners. However, a comprehensive description of what it would entail and processes by which students in distinct contexts can acquire it must be developed by critical peace educators in order to promote the necessary union of hope and action towards peace. Hence, the role of research in the field of peace education is paramount for advancing our ability to inform and generalize, rather than prescribe, processes that enable students to think and act collectively towards greater peace and social justice.

The dialectical tension between structure and agency challenges the idealistic promise of transformative agency, but does not discount its value as a construct essential to envisioning social change. While larger political, economic, and historical forces may preclude the realization of students' agency once cultivated, scholars and practitioners in peace education must attend to the obstacles in schools *and in society* in order to advance the goals of informed action for social change. Hence, collective action and radical peace politics become integral components of critical peace education though they may constitute different agendas depending on their context. Approaches that fail to question the status quo and examine the structural causes of social conflict usually accommodate the economically and politically privileged. Radical change need not be violent in order to be effective and to address social inequalities whose persistence precludes any possibility for comprehensive peace.

The conceptual foundations of peace education must be reexamined in order to tease out issues of power, domination, and symbolic violence or cultural imposition, particularly in multiethnic classrooms so as not to strip students of their agency rather than enabling it. As Gur-Ze'ev (2001) notes, generalized proclamations about peace education actually may *produce the violence* that seeks to be eliminated. While the default point of reference for many peace education scholars is the West, critical peace educators must understand local realities and resist the temptation to universalize, ignoring often distinct material and social conditions.

Metanarratives about the nature of peace and violence ignore local conceptions, unique histories, and contextualized struggles. Research about local meanings of peace and initiatives that seek to advance it can inform a scholarly body of literature from which tentative theoretical generalizations might be made. The *Journal of Peace Education*, launched in 2004, represents a significant step towards greater scholarly rigor in the field (Synott, 2005). The growing use of the term "peace education" for various scholarly and programmatic endeavors lacking any commonality otherwise requires the development of certain concepts, such as transformative agency or optimism (Rossatto, 2005), than can engage the discipline and provide some definition to its now fluid boundaries.

The transformative potential of peace education to engage learners in action towards greater equity and social justice can and ought to be galvanized through consideration of the larger social and political realities which structure, limit, and enable research and practice in the field. Questions of method need to be addressed both based on the context under study and vis-à-vis the underlying principles of peace education to promote greater social justice and equity. Ethical considerations must be paramount for researchers *and* practitioners in the field of peace education given the often wide gulf between intentions and impact.

CONCLUSION

The call for a reclaimed critical peace education is not an attempt to splinter the field, but rather a recommendation for scholars and practitioners considering peace education research. Moving away from a one-size-fits-all approach towards a contextualized and situated perspective on peace education can only further enhance the legitimacy and validity of the knowledge generated in the field. The following suggestions point towards renewed attention to critical peace education:

- Depth rather than breadth should be the aim of the critical peace education endeavor. Generalizations, rather than prescriptions, can and should emerge through greater research and methodological rigor in peace education.

- Human rights, and the debates surrounding them, should not be treated as static and fixed. Instead, students should be taught the complexities and messiness of the human rights system in ways that empower them to engage with larger international standards. The primacy of the nation state, the limitations of enforcement, and the Western biases in human rights discourse should be interrogated by students in age- and level-appropriate ways in order to foster constructive engagement rather than disillusionment.

- Marginalized groups, such as refugees and ethnic minorities, should not be the exclusive target of peace education interventions. Peace education that seeks to "normalize" or "restore" a perceived sense of social cohesion without analyses of the underlying structural roots of conflict risks exacerbating, rather than addressing, violence.

- Transformative agency, rooted in Freirean critical consciousness and praxis, should be investigated and cultivated by researchers, practitioners, and participants in ways relevant to the respective economic, political, historical, and social contexts. Structural and macro-level constraints to the realization of such agency should be discussed, analyzed, and constructively addressed in order to advance equality, participation, and social justice.

- Research and practice should attend to asymmetrical power relationships that exist in supposedly neutral spaces. Accordingly, the involvement of participants in educational and research projects should be sought at all levels to ensure ongoing evaluation, reflection, and attention to the potential peril of such initiatives. Consistent and thorough participation will also democratize both the educational and research process. The aim of peace education must include the development of "power literacy" or the ability to analyze the complex interplay among those occupying differential sites of power (Kincheloe, 2002, p. 119).

• Researchers should develop methods suited to the context under study such that the process of research does not *impose* violence, and so that the agency of both researcher and respondents is enhanced through the investigative process. In this way, critical peace education can pursue the emancipatory promise that scholars of critical research in education have elaborated as the outcome of the research endeavor (Denzin & Lincoln, 2000).

These recommendations offer scholars insights into the nature of inquiry and how, as a field, we may address the confusion that exists about what peace education is, does, and offers to educational scholarship and practice.

Presently, peace education scholarship, teaching, and practice appear to bifurcate into two camps: one calling for greater universality (Lenhart & Savolainen, 2002; Lin, 2006) and the other suggesting greater attention to realities at the local level (Salomon & Nevo, 2002; Vasquez, 1976). This split between the normative and the scientific need not be mutually exclusive (Vasquez, 1976), but requires the attention of scholars and practitioners since each perspective implies distinct analyses and worldviews. This chapter favors the latter approach towards greater scholarly rigor in the field of peace education given its potential for addressing increasingly complex manifestations of all forms of violence across the globe today. A renewed critical peace education can provide the analytical and methodological strategies to examine the causes and dimensions of social, political, and economic conflicts in their settings. By providing greater definition of the boundaries of what is and what is not peace education, scholars and practitioners of the increasingly interdisciplinary field can work together with increased momentum towards the promise of greater justice and equity within and outside of schools.

NOTES

1. Wulf (1974) and Diaz-Soto (2005) provide explanations of what constitutes "critical peace education" while Montgomery (2005) and Mirra (2008) use a "critical peace education perspective" to call for a more politicized approach.
2. "Positive peace," by contrast, addresses issues of social and economic justice with regard to the underlying structural roots of violence in all of its forms (Galtung, 1969).

REFERENCES

Althusser, L. (1979). *Reading capital*. London: Verso.

Aronowitz, S., & Giroux, H. (1993). *Education still under siege*. Westport, CT: Greenwood.

Bajaj, M. I. (2004). Human rights education and student self-conception in the Dominican Republic. *Journal of Peace Education, 1*(1), 21-36.

Bourdieu, P., & Passeron, J. (1977). *Reproduction in education, society and culture*. London: Sage.

Bowles, S., & Gintis, H. (1976). *Schooling in capitalist America*. London: Routledge.

Burns, R. J., & Aspelagh, R. (1983). Concepts of peace education: A view of western experience. *International Review of Education, 29*(3), 311–330.

Denzin, N. K., & Lincoln, Y. S. (2000). *Handbook of qualitative research* (2nd ed.). Thousand Oaks, CA: Sage.

Diaz-Soto, L. (2005). How can we teach peace when we are so outraged? A call for critical peace education. *Taboo: The Journal of Culture and Education, Fall-Winter, 9*(2), 91-96.

Freire, P. (1970). *Pedagogy of the oppressed*. New York: Continuum.

Galtung, J. (1969). Violence, peace, and peace research. *Journal of Peace Research, 6*(3), 167-191.

Giroux, H. (1988). *Schooling and the struggle for public life: Critical pedagogy in the modern age*. Minneapolis: University of Minnesota Press.

Giroux, H. (1997). *Pedagogy and the politics of hope*. Boulder, CO: Westview Press.

Gur Ze'ev, I. (2001). Philosophy of peace education in a postmodern era. *Educational Theory, 51*(3), 315-336.

Haavelsrud, M. (1996). *Education in developments*. Norway: Arena.

Harber, C. (2004). *Schooling as violence*. London: Routledge.

Harris, I. (2004). Peace education theory. *Journal of Peace Education, 1*(1), 5-20.

Ignatieff, M. (2000, April). *Human rights as politics*. Paper presented at The Tanner Lectures on Human Values at Princeton University, NJ.

Inter-agency Network for Education in Emergencies. (2005). *Peace education programme*. Retrieved November 6, 2007, from http://www.ineesite.org/page.asp?pid=1008

Kincheloe, J. (2002). *The sign of the burger: McDonalds and the culture of power*. Philadelphia: Temple University Press.

Knight, F. (2005). The Haitian Revolution and the notion of human rights. *The Journal of the Historical Society, V*(3), 391-416.

Lenhart, V., & Savolainen, K. (2002). Human rights education as a field of practice and theoretical reflection. *International Review of Education, 48*(3-4), 145-158.

Lin, J. (2006). *Love, peace, and wisdom in education: A vision for education in the 21st century*. Lanham, MD: Rowman & Littlefield.

Mamdani, M. (2002). *When victims become killers: Colonialism, nativism, and the genocide in Rwanda*. Princeton, NJ: Princeton University Press.

Mirra, C. (2008). *U.S. foreign policy and the prospects for peace education*. Jefferson, NC: McFarland Press.

Montgomery, K. (2006). Racialized hegemony and nationalist mythologies: Representations of war and peace in high school history textbooks, 1945-2005. *Journal of Peace Education, 3*(1), 19-37.

Prasad, S. N. (1998). Development of peace education in India (since independence). *Peace Education Mini Prints, 95*, 1-14.

Reardon, B. (1988). *Comprehensive peace education.* New York: Teachers College Press.

Reardon, B. (1997). Human rights as education for peace. In G. Andreopoulos & R. P. Claude (Eds.), *Human rights education for the twenty first century* (pp. 21-34). Philadelphia: University of Pennsylvania Press.

Reardon, B. (2001). *Education for a culture of peace in a gender perspective.* Paris, France: UNESCO.

Rieff, D. (1999). A new age of liberal imperialism? *World Policy Journal, 16*(2), 1-10.

Rossatto, C. A. (2005). *Engaging Paulo Freire's Pedagogy of Possibility.* Oxford, England: Rowman and Littlefield.

Salomon, G., & Baruch, N. (2002). *Peace education: the concept, principles, and practices around the world.* London: Erlbaum.

Spener, D. (1990). *The Freirean approach to adult literacy education.* National Center for ESL Literacy Education 1990. Retrieved April 25 2007, from http://www.cal.org/caela/esl_resources/digests/FREIREQA.html

Synott, J. (2005). Peace education as an educational paradigm: review of a changing field using an old measure. *Journal of Peace Education, 2*(1), 3-16.

United Nations. (2007). *United Nations encyclopedia.* Retrieved April 25 2007, from http://www.history.com/encyclopedia.do?articleId=224820#fw.un009200.a.t010.r100

Vasquez, J. A. (1976). Toward a unified strategy for peace education: Resolving the two cultures problem in the classroom. *The Journal of Conflict Resolution, 20*(4), 707-728.

Willis, P. (1977). *Learning to labor: How working class kids get working class jobs.* New York: Columbia University Press.

Wintersteiner, W. (1999). *Pedagogy of the other: Building blocks for peace education in the postmodern world.* Munster, Ireland: Agenda.

Wulf, C. (1974). *Handbook of peace education.* Frankfurt, Germany: International Peace Research Association.

CHAPTER 17

UNITY-BASED
PEACE EDUCATION

H. B. Danesh

INTRODUCTION

The conceptual dilemma of peace education is most consequential. Many theories of peace use conflict as their point of departure and the cessation of violence (negative peace) as their dominant objective. This focus on conflict as an inherent and therefore an unavoidable and even necessary aspect of human life has had far-reaching consequences, the most important of which regards the orientation of the discipline of peace studies and the effectiveness of peace education programs. By placing "conflict" at the core of theories of peace and "conflict management" as their ultimate objective, the discipline of peace studies has abandoned its primary raison d'etre—to study the nature of peace and the dynamics of peace building. Most theories of peace do not place adequate emphasis on the process of peace building and the development of the inherent capacities of individuals, institutions, communities, civil society, and governments, both to prevent violence and to create harmonious relationships. Furthermore, the current conceptual formulations of peace studies and peace education pay little or no attention to the all-important

Encyclopedia of Peace Education, pp. 147–156

task of building a civilization of peace—peaceful and just, united and diverse, prosperous and benevolent, technologically advanced and environmentally healthy, intellectually rich and morally sound.

A careful review of current thought on the causes of conflict and violence shows that certain basic assumptions form the foundation of most existing theories with regard to the phenomena of human conflict in all its varied expressions—intrapersonal, interpersonal, and intergroup. These assumptions basically focus on issues of survival, security, pleasure, and individual and/or group identity; consider interpersonal/intergroup power-struggle and intense competition as necessary and inevitable life processes; and deem conflict the unavoidable outcome of this struggle (Dahrendorf, 1958; Coser cited in Wehr, 2001). According to these theories, the best we could accomplish is to decrease the destructiveness of human conflict and develop tools to resolve conflicts before they turn into aggression and violence. Within this overriding prominence accorded to "conflict" in most peace-related theories and action, there have been notable efforts on the part of various researchers and practitioners to offset the unavoidable negative consequences of conflict. Among these are several concepts and approaches to conflict resolution such as "super-ordinate goals" (Deutsch, 1973; Galtung & Jacobsen, 2000; Worchel, 1986), cooperative conflict resolution (Deutsch, 1994; Johnson, Johnson, & Tjosvold, 2000), principled negotiation (Fisher, Ury, & Patton, 1991), conflict transformation (Bush & Opp, 2001; Lederach, 1995) and stable peace (Boulding, 1977, 1978, 1991; Galtung, 1996).

During the course of the past decade, a new and challenging perspective on peace and conflict has been proposed, defining unity as the main law governing all human relationships and conflict as the absence of unity. Based on these concepts, an integrative theory of peace (ITP) has been offered and a comprehensive unity-based peace education program—education for peace (EFP)—has been formulated and successfully implemented in over 100 schools, involving some 80,000 students and thousands of teachers and parents in Bosnia and Herzegovina (BiH) (Clarke-Habibi, 2005; Danesh 1986, 2002, & 2006; Danesh & Danesh 2002a, 2002b, 2004).

THE INTEGRATIVE THEORY OF PEACE

ITP is based on the concept that peace is, at once, a psychological, social, political, ethical, and spiritual state with expressions at intrapersonal, interpersonal, intergroup, international, and global areas of human life.

ITP holds that all human states of being, including peace, are the outcome of the main human cognitive (knowing), emotive (loving), and conative (choosing) capacities, which together determine the nature of our worldview. ITP draws from the existing body of research on issues of psychosocial development and peace education, developmental approach to conflict resolution, and the lessons learned and observations made during seven years of implementation of the EFP in 112 schools in BiH. ITP consists of four subtheories:

- Peace is a psychosocial, political as well as a moral and spiritual condition;
- Peace is the main expression of a unity-based worldview;
- A unity-based worldview is the prerequisite for creating both a culture of peace and culture of healing;
- A comprehensive, integrated, and lifelong education is the most effective approach for development of a unity-based worldview.

Additionally, ITP posits that peace has its roots in the:

- Satisfaction of human needs for survival, safety and security;
- Human quest for freedom, justice, and interconnectedness;
- Human search for meaning, purpose, and righteousness.

The theory further holds that peace is the finest fruit of the human individual and social maturation process. It is the ultimate outcome of our transition from self-centered and anxiety-ridden insecurities of survival instincts and the quarrelsome, dichotomous tensions of identity-formation processes to a universal and all-inclusive state of awareness of our fundamental oneness and connectedness with all humanity and, in fact, with all life.

Three concepts, described below, form the foundations of ITP: unity, worldview, and human individual, and collective development.

The Concept of Unity

The concept of unity states that unity, not conflict, is the central governing law of life and that once unity is established, conflicts are often prevented or easily resolved. Unity is defined as:

a conscious and purposeful condition of convergence of two or more unique entities in a state of harmony, integration, and cooperation to create a new evolving entity(s), usually, of a same or a higher level of integration and complexity. (Danesh & Danesh, 2002a, p. 67)

The animating force of unity is love, which is expressed variably in different conditions of existence. This definition states that unity in all its expressions—psychological, social, and moral—is a deliberate phenomenon and not a chance occurrence devoid of intention, purpose, and informed operation. We have the option to create unity and conditions conducive to life or to do the opposite. As soon as the law of unity is violated, conflict with all its destructive properties shapes our intrapersonal, interpersonal, and social processes and relationships. In brief, *conflict is the absence of unity and disunity is the source and cause of conflict.*

The Concept of Worldview

Worldview has been variably defined, often within three different frameworks: mechanistic, organismic, and contextualistic.

- The mechanistic worldview sees both the individual and the world, as well as the dynamics of their respective development and change, within a mechanical and machine-like framework;
- The organismic worldview sees the world as a living organism in a constant state of change, adaptation, and modification;
- The contextualistic worldview considers all human behavior to have meaning and to be open to comprehension within a specific social–historical context (Miller, 1999).

In the ITP and EFP literature, the concept of worldview refers to our view of reality, human nature, the purpose of life, and the character and quality of human relationships. The all-important issues of personal and group narrative and identity formation that play a significant role with respect to both conflict and peace are important aspects of this formulation of worldview (Bar-Tal, 2000, 2002; Salomon, 2002, 2006). Our worldviews are formed by our respective life experiences, education, and unique individual endowments and creativity. Of these three foci of influence on worldview development, the role of education is especially significant because, in the final analysis, education has a profound impact on how we both respond to and shape our life experiences. Every society determines the focus, philosophy, and scope of education it provides for its children and youth at home, in the school, and through community resources, particularly those of religion, culture, and history. It is within the framework of our worldviews that we understand ourselves, explain events, and interpret the words and deeds of others. Our worldviews also influence our philosophical perspectives and scientific formulations and paradigms.

Three metacategories of worldview—survival-based, identity-based, and unity-based—are identified within the parameters of psychosocial developmental stages roughly corresponding to those of childhood, adolescence, and adulthood. Both survival-based and identity-based worldviews revolve around the issue of power—dominance and power-struggle, respectively—and are highly prone to conflict and violence. The main

Table 17.1.   Characteristics of the Three Metacategories of Worldview

Survival-Based Worldview	Identity-Based Worldview	Unity-Based Worldview
• Normal during childhood; • Corresponds to the agrarian and pre-industrial periods of societal development; • Develops under conditions of poverty, injustice, anarchy, physical threat, and war; • Life processes are viewed as being dangerous; • Dichotomous views of human nature as either bad (weak) or good (strong) and human beings are viewed as good or evil; • The main purpose of life is survival; • All relationships take place in the context of domination and submission—proclivity to use force and/or conformity; • Conflict and violence are inevitable; • Authoritarianism is the main mode of leadership and governance.	• Normal during adolescence; • Corresponds to the gradual coming of age of both the individual and the society; • Is particularly prevalent during emergence from authoritarian and/or revolutionary circumstances and rapid social change; • Life is viewed as an arena of the "survival of the fittest"; • Individualistic view of human nature with focus on individualism and group-identities—ethnicity, nationality, race, religion, and so forth; • The main purpose of life is to "have" and to "win," which corresponds with the notion of human nature as greedy and selfish; • All relationships operate within the parameters of extremes of competition and rivalry; • Conflict is viewed as inherent in human nature and necessary for progress; • Adversarial Democracy is the main mode of leadership and governance.	• Normal during adulthood; • Corresponds with the phase of maturity of humanity based on the consciousness of the oneness of humanity; • Is the next stage in human individual and collective development; • Life is seen as the process of unity-building; • Views human nature to be potentially noble, creative and integrative, and highly responsive to the forces of nature and nurture; • Views the main purpose of human life as the creation of a civilization of peace—equal, just, liberal, moral, diverse, and united; • All relationships operate within the parameters of the law of unity in the context of diversity; • Conflict is viewed as the absence of unity; • An integrated unity-based democracy is seen to be emerging as the main mode of leadership and governance (Danesh, 2002, 2006).

characteristics of these three metacategories of worldview are summarized in Table 17.1 for ease of access.

The Concept of Individual and Collective Development

The subject of human development has been the focal point of many researchers and theorists, among them Freud (1940), Piaget (1960), Erikson (1968), Flavell (1999), Bandura (1977), and many others. These theories are primarily concerned with the development of the individual and, secondarily address the dynamics of development of social entities and focus on biological as well as environmental and experiential dimensions of human development.

The environmental and experiential aspects of development refer to the monumental human capacity for learning, thinking, and self-awareness—in brief, human consciousness. Human development takes place on the axis of consciousness, which shapes both our worldview and the manner in which we engage in the task of influencing and changing our environments. Thus, over time, we develop a greater understanding of ourselves, of other human beings, of nature, and of reality in all its varied expressions. This new understanding, in turn, modifies our behavior toward self, others, and the environment, and helps us to continuously refine the nature of all our relationships. The normal direction of the development of worldview is toward ever-higher levels of integration and unity. The two main engines of human development are science, which discovers fundamental laws that govern all natural phenomena, and religion that enunciates and elucidates spiritual laws that inform us of the purpose and direction of human life.

Development of human consciousness has integrative and creative qualities and its beneficial outcomes affect all involved—the individual, the society, and the environment. In this creative cycle, the development of the individual contributes to the advancement of the society which, in turn, facilitates the process of individual development. It is here that the true power of the individual resides and the capacity of society to empower its members is expressed.

EDUCATION FOR PEACE

Based on the main concepts of the ITP, in the course of the past decade (1997-2007) several unity-based peace programs have been developed, including conflict-free conflict resolution (CFCR) (Danesh & Danesh, 2002a, 2002b, 2004) and EFP (Clarke-Habibi, 2005; Danesh 2006;

Danesh & Clarke-Habibi, 2007). In September 1999, a CFCR workshop was held in Sarajevo, BiH. Among the participants were BiH government officials, members of the international community in that country, and many journalists. The BiH participants were members of the three main ethnic populations of the country who had been engaged in the bitter and calamitous civil war of 1992-1995. Because of the positive outcome of the workshop, an invitation was extended by the government and international officials to the International Education for Peace Institute to bring their EFP program to the BiH schools.

The EFP program is a comprehensive and integrative program of peace education for primary and secondary schools. The program was initially piloted in six (three primary and three secondary) schools in BiH and later was extended to a total of 112 schools in that country. These schools together have some 80,000 students, 5,000 teachers and thousands of parents from the three main ethnic BiH populations—Bosniak (Muslim), Croat (Catholic), and Serb (Orthodox Christian)—who were engaged in the violent civil war of 1992-1995. These school communities are located in 65 villages, towns, and cities across the country.

Four conditions are identified by ITP for a successful program of peace education: a unity-based worldview, a culture of peace, a culture of healing, and a peace-based curriculum for all educational activities. Based on these conditions, the EFP program focuses on four main tasks: (a) to assist all members of the school community to reflect on their own worldviews and to gradually try to develop a peace-based worldview; (b) to assist all participants to embark on the creation of a culture of peace in and between their school communities; (c) to create a culture of healing with the capacity to help its members to gradually, but effectively, recover from the damages of protracted conflict affecting themselves, their families, and community members; and (d) to learn how to successfully prevent new conflicts and resolve them in a peaceful manner, without resorting to violence, once they have occurred.

The process of worldview transformation from conflict-orientation to peace-orientation is the framework within which all prerequisites of EFP are met and its main objectives are achieved. In this context, the *culture of peace* refers to an environment in which the principles of equality, justice, individual and group safety and security, and freedom in the context of ethical, lawful, and democratic practices are the norm. The *culture of healing* is characterized by the principles of truth and truthfulness, trust and trustworthiness, empathy and cooperation, fairness and fair mindedness, forgiveness and reconciliation at interpersonal and intergroup levels. In the course of the application of the EFP program in BiH schools, it was demonstrated that once a culture of peace and a culture of healing in and between the participating schools is created, a third beneficial outcome—

a *culture of excellence*—emerges. The culture of excellence refers to an environment that encourages and facilitates high levels of accomplishment by all members of the school community in academic, artistic, behavioral, ethical, and skills aspects of their respective learning endeavors.

The EFP integrative curriculum is designed to be both *universal* and *specific*. The universality of the curriculum refers to the universal principles of peace—the common heritage of humanity, the diverse expression of this common heritage, and the absolute necessity to create a unified and peaceful world within this framework of oneness and diversity without resorting to conflict and violence. While the principles of peace education are universal, their implementation is context-specific. For each distinct society, the EFP-international faculty, in close collaboration with the educators and experts from that community, designs a specific version of the EFP curriculum with due consideration of the unique characteristics, needs, and challenges of that community.

The EFP integrative curriculum is designed in a flexible format, allowing it to evolve and be modified in light of new research findings and insights gained in the course of implementation of the EFP curriculum and other peace education programs in schools around the world. The EFP curriculum consists of 10 interrelated but independent books that together, comprise a comprehensive and integrative peace education curriculum. The curriculum is formulated to provide a framework within which all subjects—literature, history, math, biology, sociology, and music, and so forth—are explored. Teachers trained in the EFP program become familiar with the principles of peace and learn how to integrate these principles into their daily lessons and activities with students through the use of EFP's "understanding-oriented" approach. Through exploration of the broad principles and concepts of peace, students develop the ability to contextualize information and data in each of their subject areas, and to connect learning in one area with relevant issues in other fields.

The EFP curriculum is interdisciplinary in its approach and draws from various fields of study as they apply to the issue of peace at intrapersonal, interpersonal, intergroup, and international levels. The curriculum is based on the latest research and literature on peace education, as well as insights drawn from the fields of psychology, education methodology, political science, sociology, law, religious studies, history, conflict resolution, the arts, and other peace-related fields.

CONCLUSION

Unity-based peace education is an emerging new approach to the field of peace studies with regard to both its conceptual and practical dimensions.

ITP, which considers unity as the main law of life and the central force for creation of peace, rejects the primacy of the role of conflict in this field. ITP holds that conflict is the absence of unity and both conflict resolution and peace creation are only possible in the context of a unity-based worldview. One outstanding example of unity-based peace education is the EFP program which has been successfully applied to many schools with thousands of students in the highly divided postconflict societies of BiH and is now being gradually introduced into schools in other parts of the world.

REFERENCES

Bandura, A. (1977). *Social learning theory.* New York: General Learning Press.

Bar-Tal, D. (2002). The elusive nature of peace education. In G. Salomon & B. Nevo (Eds.), *Peace education: The concept, principles, and practices around the world* (pp. 27-36). Mahwah, NJ: Erlbaum.

Bar-Tal, D. (2000). *Shared beliefs in a society.* Thousand Oaks, CA: Sage

Boulding, K. (1977). Twelve friendly quarrels with Johan Galtung. *Journal of Peace Research, 14*(1), 75-86.

Boulding, K. (1978). Future directions of conflict and peace studies. *The Journal of Conflict Resolution, 22*(2), 342-354.

Boulding, K. (1991). Stable peace among nations: A learning process. In E. Boulding, C. Brigagao, & K. Clements, (Eds.). *Peace, culture and society: Transnational research and dialogue* (pp. 108-14). Boulder, CO: Westview Press.

Bush, K. D., & Opp, R. J. (2001). *Peace and conflict impact assessment.* International Development Research Centre. Retrieved November 6, from http://www.idrc.ca/en/ev-27981-201-1-DO_TOPIC.html

Clarke-Habibi, S. (2005). Transforming worldviews: The case of Education for Peace. *Journal of Transformative Education, 3*(1), 33-56.

Dahrendorf, R. (1958). Toward a theory of social conflict. *Journal of Conflict Resolution, 2,* 170-83.

Danesh, H. B. (1986). *Unity: The creative foundation of peace.* Ottawa and Toronto, Canada: Bahá'i Studies Publications and Fitzhenry & Whiteside.

Danesh, H. B. (2002) Breaking the cycle of violence: Education for peace. In *African civil society organization and development: Re-Evaluation for the 21st century* (pp. 32-39). New York: United Nations.

Danesh, H. B. (2006) Towards an integrative theory of peace education. *Journal of Peace Education, 3*(1), 55-78.

Danesh, H. B., & Clarke-Habibi, S. (2007). *Education for peace curriculum manual.* Neuchâtel, Switzerland: EFP-International.

Danesh H. B., & Danesh, R. P. (2002a). Has conflict resolution grown up?: Toward a new model of decision making and conflict resolution. *International Journal of Peace Studies, 7*(1), 59-76. Retrieved November 6, 2007, from http://www.gmu.edu/academic/ijps/vol7_1/Danesh.html

Danesh H. B., & Danesh, R. P. (2002b). A consultative conflict resolution model: beyond alternative dispute-resolution. *International Journal of Peace Studies*, 7(2), 17-33.

Danesh H. B., & Danesh, R. P (2004). Conflict-free conflict resolution: Process and methodology. *Peace and Conflict Studies*, 11(2), 55-84.

Deutsch, M. (1973). *The resolution of conflict: Constructive and destructive processes.* New Haven, CT: Yale University Press.

Deutsch, M. (1994). Constructive conflict resolution: Principals, training and research. *Journal of Social Issues*, 50, 13–32.

Erikson, E. (1968). *Identity, youth, and crisis.* New York: W. W. Norton.

Fisher, R., Ury, W., & Patton, B. (1991). *Getting to yes: Negotiating agreement without giving in* (2nd ed). New York: Penguin Books.

Flavell, J. H. (1999). Cognitive development: Children's knowledge about the mind. *Annual Review of Psychology*, 16, 21.

Freud, S. (1940). *An outline of psychoanalysis.* New York: W. W. Norton.

Galtung, J., & Jacobsen, C. G. (2000). *Searching for peace: The road to TRANSCEND.* London: Pluto Press.

Galtung, J. (1996). *Peace by peaceful means: Peace and conflict, development and civilisation.* Oslo, Norway: PRIO.

Johnson, D., Johnson, R., & Tjosvold, D. (2000). Constructive controversy: The value of intellectual opposition. In M. Deutsch & P. T. Coleman (Eds.), *The handbook of conflict resolution: Theory and practice.* San Francisco: Jossey-Bass.

Lederach, J. P. (1995). *Preparing for peace: Conflict transformation across cultures.* Syracuse, New York: Syracuse University Press. Retrieved November 12, 2007, from http://spot.colorado.edu/~wehr/40RD2.TXT

Miller, P. (1999). *Theories of developmental psychology* (3rd ed). New York: W. H. Freeman.

Piaget, J. (1960). *The child's conception of the world.* Paterson, NJ: Littlefield, Adams.

Salomon, G. (2002). The nature of peace education: Not all programs are equal. In G. Salomon & B. Nevo (Eds.), *Peace education: The concept, principles, and practices around the world.* Mahwah, NJ: Erlbaum.

Salomon, G (2006). Does peace education really make a difference? *Peace and Conflict: Journal of Peace Psychology*, 12(1), 37-48.

Wehr, P. (2001). *Conflict theory and analytic sociology.* University of Colorado at Boulder Department of Sociology course chapter. Retrieved November 12, 2007, from http://spot.colorado.edu/~wehr/40RD2.TXT

Worchel, S. (1986). The role of cooperation in reducing intergroup conflict. In S. Worchel & W. G. Austin (Eds.), *Psychology of Intergroup Relations* (pp. 288-304). Chicago: Nelson-Hall.

ABOUT THE AUTHORS

Monisha Bajaj is assistant professor of education in the Department of International and Transcultural Studies at Teachers College, Columbia University. Her research and teaching interests include peace and human rights education, and educational policy and practice in diverse international and U.S. contexts such as Zambia, India, the Dominican Republic, and New York City. She has recently initiated a new project to study human rights education programs for Dalit or untouchable children in southern India. Dr. Bajaj has also developed curriculum on peace and human rights education for UNESCO, UNICEF, and various NGOs in the United States and abroad.

Lesley Bartlett is an associate professor affiliated with the programs in International and Comparative Education and Anthropology of Education at Teachers College, Columbia University. Her research and teaching interests include critical pedagogy, sociocultural studies of literacy, race and class inequality, and immigration. She is the author of a forthcoming book titled, *The Word and the World: The Cultural Politics of Literacy in Brazil.*

Robin Burns established the first Australian peace education course in the early 1980s within university teacher education, following her doctoral dissertation on a comparative study of development education in nine nations. She has always argued for strong links between the teaching of key social, political, and economic issues such as peace, development, justice, human rights and equity. From 1983-6 she was the executive secretary of the Peace Education Commission (PEC) of the International Peace Research Association. With the preceding PEC executive secretary, Robert

Aspeslagh of The Netherlands, she coedited *Three Decades of Peace Education around the World* (New York: Garland, 1996). Since retiring from La Trobe University she has focused on a long-term project on scientific fieldwork in remote areas (Antarctica, Uzbekistan, the Namib Desert, the Altai Republic), as Adjunct Associate Professor of Public Health at La Trobe on a project on emergency risk management, and on a book on ageing and caring for the aged. She maintains an interest in comparative and social education, justice issues and conservation, teaches voluntary courses at the University of the Third Age, and revels in adventure travel.

H. B. Danesh, MD, FRCP (C) is the founder and president of the International Education for Peace Institute and the first President of Landegg International University (1998-2003), in Switzerland. He is a visiting professor of peace education and conflict resolution at the European Peace University, Austria; a consultant on "leadership" to the United Nations Development Program in Southern Africa (2005-2006) and associate professor of psychiatry at the University of Ottawa (1973-1985). He is one of the founders of the Association for Baha'i Studies. Dr. Danesh is the author or coauthor of the *11-Volume Education for Peace Integrative Curriculum* and five other books including *Unity: The Creative Foundation of Peace, The Violence-Free Society: A Gift for Our Children, The Psychology of Spirituality: from divided self to integrated self,* and *The Violence-Free Family: Building Block of a Peaceful Civilization,* in addition to many articles in his areas of specialization.

Lynn Davies is professor of International Education in the Centre for International Education and Research (CIER) at the School of Education, University of Birmingham. Her major teaching, research, and consultancy interests are in educational management internationally, particularly concerning democracy, citizenship, gender and human rights. She takes a specific focus on conflict and education, in terms of how education contributes to conflict and/or to peace or civil renewal. Related work has been in Angola, Sri Lanka, Kosovo, Bosnia, Palestine, Malawi and the Gambia, as well as with UNESCO on their Associated Schools. Current research projects are on school improvement in post-conflict Angola; education for peace and social cohesion in Sri Lanka; and the work of student councils in school improvement. Her book *Education and Conflict: Complexity and Chaos* (2004) was awarded the Society for Education Studies prize for the best book of 2004. Her new book *Educating Against Extremism* will be published by Trentham in Spring 2008.

Cheryl Duckworth is a teacher, student, peace-building program leader and conflict resolution policy analyst who has served such organizations as the Institute for Multi-Track Diplomacy, the Center for International Education and InterAction. She has lived in Zimbabwe and Paraguay, and her policy work has focused on peace education, human rights, global security, democratic governance, and policies for ending poverty. She has published and presented globally. She is currently completing her doctoral dissertation on the indigenous rights movement in Paraguay at the Institute for Conflict Analysis and Resolution, George Mason University and teaches at the Northern VA Juvenile Detention Center.

Johan Galtung is founder and director of TRANSCEND—*A Peace and Development Network for Conflict Transformation by Peaceful Means*, with more than 300 members from over 80 countries around the world and Rector of TRANSCEND Peace University (TPU). An experienced peace worker and professor of peace studies, he is widely regarded as the founder of the academic discipline of peace research and one of the leading pioneers of peace and conflict transformation in theory and practice. He has played an active role in helping mediate and prevent violence in 45 major conflicts around the world over the past four decades, and is author of the United Nations' first ever manual for trainers and participants on "Conflict Transformation by Peaceful Means: The TRANSCEND Approach" (UNDP, 2000). He has taught peace studies at the Universities of Hawai'i, Witten/Herdecke, Tromsoe, Alicante, Ritsumeikan and the European Peace University, among many others. Galtung established the Peace Research Institute, Oslo (PRIO) in 1959, the *Journal of Peace Research* in 1964, and colaunched the Nordic Institute for Peace Research (NIFF) in 2000. He has published more than 1000 articles covering a wide-range of fields, including peaceful conflict transformation, deep culture, peace pedagogy, reconciliation, development, peace building and empowerment, global governance, direct structural and cultural peace/violence, peace journalism, and reflections on current events, and more than 100 books translated into dozens of languages. His most recent books include *Transcend and Transform* (Pluto Press, 2004), *Searching for Peace the Road to TRANSCEND* (Pluto, 2000 & 2002), *Peace by Peaceful Means: Peace and Conflict, Development and Civilization* (SAGE, 1996), *Collective Essays on Peace Research and Methodology* (Christian Ejlers, Copenhagen) *60 Speeches on War and Peace* (PRIO, 1990).

Magnus Haavelsrud is a professor of education at the Norwegian University of Science and Technology in Trondheim, Norway. His work deals with the critique of the reproductive role of education and the possibilities for transcendence of this reproduction in light of the traditions of educational sociology and peace research. He took part in the creation of the Peace Education Commission of the International Peace Research

Association at the beginning of the 70s and served as the Commissions 2nd Executive Secretary 1975-79. He was the program chair for the World Conference on Education in 1974 and edited the proceeding from this conference titled *Education for Peace: Reflection and Action*. He served as the Carl-von-Ossietzky Guest Professor of the German Council for Peace and Conflict Research. His publications include: *Education in Developments* (1996), *Perspektiv i utdanningssosiologi* (Perspectives in the Sociology of Education (1997, 2nd edition), *Education Within the Archipelago of Peace Research 1945-1964*, (coauthored with Mario Borrelli, 1993), *Disarming: Discourse on Violence and Peace* (editor, 1993) and *Approaching Disarmament Education* (editor, 1981).

Ian Harris is a professor emeritus from the Department of Educational Policy and Community Studies at the University of Wisconsin-Milwaukee. He is author of the book, *Peace Education*, and founder of the *Journal of Peace Education*. He also serves as president of the International Peace Research Association Foundation.

David Hicks is visiting professor at the School of Education, Bath Spa University, United Kingdom. He is internationally recognized for his work on the need for a global and futures dimension in the curriculum and is particularly interested in ways of helping students and teachers think more critically and creatively about the future. He has published widely in the fields of futures education, global education, and previously peace education. His most recent books are *Teaching the Global Dimension: Key Principles and Effective Practice*, with Cathie Holden (RoutledgeFalmer, 2007), and *Lessons for the Future: The Missing Dimension in Education* (Trafford Publishing, 2005).

Charles F. Howlett teaches in the graduate program, education division, at Molloy College. He received his degrees from Marist College, the University at Albany, and Columbia. He is a former Fulbright Scholar to the Netherlands and a Woodrow Wilson Foundation Teaching Fellow. He is the author or coauthor of seven books and over 150 articles in scholarly and popular journals. His forthcoming book, coauthored with Robbie Lieberman, is *Looking Forward: A Survey of Pioneers for Peace and Social Justice in American History*.

Carl Mirra is an associate professor in the Ruth S. Ammon School of Education at Adelphi University in Garden City, New York. He is editor of *Enduring Freedom or Enduring War? The Prospects and Costs of the New American 21st Century* (Maisonneuve Press, 2005) and author of *U.S. Foreign Policy and the Prospects for Peace Education* (McFarland Press) and is completing an oral history of the Iraq War for Palgrave/Macmillian. His articles have appeared in *Left History, American Diplomacy, Peace Review, ZNet, History News Network* and elsewhere. He holds an MA, MPhil, and PhD in history and education from Teachers College, Columbia University.

Nel Noddings is Lee L. Jacks Professor of Education, Emerita, at Stanford University. She is a past president of the National Academy of Education, the Philosophy of Education Society and the John Dewey Society. In addition to sixteen books—among them, *Caring: A Feminine Approach to Ethics and Moral* Education, *Women and Evil, The Challenge to Care in Schools, Educating for Intelligent Belief or Unbelief,* and *Philosophy of Education*—she is the author of more than 200 articles and chapters on various topics ranging from the ethics of care to mathematical problem solving. Her latest books are *Happiness and Education, Educating Citizens for Global Awareness, Critical Lessons: What Our Schools Should Teach,* and most recent *When School Reform Goes Wrong.*

James Page holds a PhD in peace education and has taught widely in Australia and overseas, including most recently with Southern Cross University and Queensland University of Technology. He is currently Australian coordinator of a research project examining social attitudes to peace and war. Dr. Page has published widely in peace education and his most recent book is *Peace Education: Exploring Ethical and Philosophical Foundations.*

Dale T. Snauwaert is associate professor of philosophy of education and director of the Center for Nonviolence and Democratic Education in the Judith Herb College of Education at the University of Toledo. He received his BA in philosophy at the University of Illinois at Chicago in 1983, a MEd in educational policy and PhD in philosophy of education from the University of Illinois at Urbana-Champaign in 1990. He has also taught at Colgate University, The University of Missouri, Teachers College, Columbia University, and Adelphi University. He is the author of *Democracy, Education, and Governance: A Developmental Conception* (State University of New York Press, 1993), which received an American Educational Studies Association Critics' Choice Award in 1995. He has published in such academic journals as *Educational Theory, Journal of Educational Thought, Peabody Journal of Education, Holistic Education Review, Current Issues in Comparative Education, The Online Journal of Peace and Conflict Resolution,* and *Encounter* on such topics as democratic education, the nature of teaching, moral education, holistic education, and international ethics. He is currently working on a book on the ethics of war and peace and human rights education with the Earth Charter as a framework. He is currently the editor of *In Factis Pax* (an online journal of peace education and social justice).

Felisa Tibbitts is director and cofounder of Human Rights Education Associates (HREA), an international nongovernmental organization dedicated to education and learning about human rights (http://www.hrea.org). She has supported national curricular reform efforts in human rights, law-related and civic education programming in Romania, Albania, Estonia, Ukraine, Croatia, Morocco and China, and has been involved in teacher trainings in 20 countries. Ms. Tibbitts has published extensively on the topic of human rights education and is a consultative expert for the Council of Europe, UNICEF, UNESCO, OSCE, the Open Society Institute and the Office of the U.N. High Commissioner for Human Rights. She is a member of the editorial board for the journal *Intercultural Education*, Amnesty International-USA's Steering Committee for Human Rights Education, and the Organization of the Americas Advisory Council on Democratic and Human Rights Education.

GLOSSARY OF TERMS

Caring theory: explanation of reciprocal relationships between a "carer" and a "cared-for," in which dialogue and mutual contribution are key; caring relationships aim to prevent conflict (Noddings, 1984/2003; Reardon, 1985; Ruddick, 1989).

Civic education: transmission of knowledge to develop a more active, informed, and engaged citizenry, and to encourage people to participate in the idea of the nation-state (United States Agency for International Development (USAID), 2002).

Comprehensive peace education: philosophy and knowledge transmission to empower people with the awareness and consciousness of violence and the skills and attitudes to create a global, humanist, and safe world within a common conceptual framework; includes and integrates other areas, including human rights education, conflict resolution, and nuclear and disarmament education (Harris & Morrison, 2003; Reardon, 2000).

Conflict resolution education: transmission of knowledge and understanding of the nature of conflict and the conflict resolution processes to settle disputes peacefully and alternative dispute resolution (Harris & Morrison, 2003; Reardon, 2000).

Cosmopolitanism: philosophy that even though there is a wide diversity of humans and cultural differences, the moral notion of humanity and common values transcend the boundaries of ideas, culture and ideologies (Appiah, 2006).

Critical consciousness (inquiry): sociopolitical notion that learners should question and challenge their historical and social conditions in order to be critically aware of oppressive situations and to work towards a more democratic society; Paulo Freire refers to this idea as "conscientization" (Freire, 1970; Stevens, n.d.).

Critical thinking: the disciplined process of conceptualizing, analyzing, and evaluating information and propositions by examining and questioning assumptions through conscious and deliberate reasoning; aim is to guide the development of beliefs to inform action (Huitt, 1998; Mertes, 1991; Scriven & Paul, 1992).

Culture of peace: set of values, attitudes, traditions, and behaviors that ascribe to the notions of freedom, justice, democracy, tolerance, solidarity, cooperation, pluralism, cultural diversity, dialogue and understanding; it also demonstrates a strong respect for all human rights, nonviolence, and fundamental freedoms; education is important to building this culture (United Nations Educational, Scientific and Cultural Organization (UNESCO), 1999).

Dialogical method: approach to learning that encourages open communication between students and teachers such that both teach and both learn; in contrast to the banking approach of education which favors lecture-style formats where students do not actively engage in the learning process (Freire, 1970, 1994; Stevens, n.d.).

Disarmament education: transmission of knowledge that creates awareness of the social, political, economic, and cultural repercussions of the production and acquisition of arms; aims to promote peace through non-proliferation (UNESCO, 1980).

Discourse: communication system that acknowledges how history and social contexts shape and construct the way in which reality is perceived and understood through language, complex signs and practices (Leistyna, Woodrum, & Sherblom, 1996).

Environmental education: transmission of knowledge about ecological violence, the degradation of local and community environments, and the holistic and interconnectedness of all things; aims to learn how to be environmentally responsible and to live within the limits of environmental sustainability (Harris & Morrison, 2003; Reardon, 2000).

Feminist education: challenges core social and cultural values that look at patriarchal violence both locally and globally and how patriarchy is connected to systemic violence; aims to promote norms of empathy and nonviolence (Brock-Utne, 1985; Harris & Morrison, 2003; Reardon, 2000).

Futures education: transmission of knowledge, understanding, and skills necessary to critically and creatively think about the future (Hicks, 2004; Hicks & Slaughter, 1988).

Global citizen: someone who takes responsibility as an active and engaged citizen of the world with an awareness of global issues, a respect for diversity, and outrage for social injustice; active in community participation to make the world more equitable (Oxfam, 2006).

Human rights education: transmission of knowledge and skills to build a universal culture that respects human rights and fundamental freedoms, believes in the full development of human potential, and promotes understanding, tolerance and equity (United Nations, 1996).

Liberatory education: transmission of knowledge that raises learners' consciousnesses to empower them to challenge oppressive social conditions; aims to prepare learners to actively engage in social struggles for liberation and justice (Freire, 1970; Stevens, n.d.).

Militarism: notion that the military culture associated with armies and wars pervades political and civic life; militaristic values, actions, and thoughts give the culture prestige and are found in all parts of civilian life (Vagts, 1981; Wahlstrom, 1991).

Multicultural education: transmission of knowledge that encourages respect for other cultures and ways of life; aims to promote a fundamental understanding of humanity (Reardon, 2000).

Negative peace: the absence of direct or physical violence; aims to prevent war, conflict, and physical violence (Galtung, 1964, 1969).

Peace education: transmission of knowledge about and skills to achieve and maintain peace, and the obstacles that stands in the way (Reardon, 2000).

Peace studies: the study of peace as a concept, as well as peace processes; focuses on causes of war and conflict, and how to avoid them (Harris & Morrison, 2003).

Planetary stewardship: the notion that every person is a caretaker of the Earth, and as such, has the responsibility to respect and care for it (Ardizzone, 2007).

Positive peace: absence of structural violence; aims to develop more democratic systems by reducing the structures that create inequality and injustice (Galtung, 1964, 1969).

Structural violence: state of social inequality in which privileged groups exploit or oppress others; created by deprivation of basic human needs, such as civil rights, health, and education (Galtung, 1969; Harris & Morrison, 2003).

Transformative optimism: outlook that structural violence can be overcome if every person sees himself or herself as a necessary and viable part of the collective process for structural change (Rossatto, 2005).

REFERENCES

Ardizzone, L. (2007). *Gettin' my word out: Voices of urban youth activists*. New York: State University of New York Press.

Appiah, K. A. (2006). *Cosmopolitanism: Ethics in a world of strangers*. New York: W. W. Norton.

Brock-Utne, B. (1985). *Educating for peace: A feminist perspective*. New York: Pergamon Press.

Freire, P. (1970). *Pedagogy of the oppressed*. New York: Continuum Press.

Freire, P. (1994). *Pedagogy of hope: Reliving pedagogy of the oppressed*. New York: Continuum.

Galtung, J. (1964). An editorial. *Journal of Peace Research, 1*(1), 1-4.

Galtung, J. (1969). Violence, peace and peace research. *Journal of Peace Research, 6*(3), 167-191.

Harris, I., & M. Morrison (2003). *Peace education* (2nd ed.). Jefferson, NC: McFarland.

Hicks, D. (2004). Teaching for tomorrow: how can futures studies contribute to peace education? *Journal of Peace Education, 1*, 165-178.

Hicks, D., & Slaughter, R. (Eds.). (1988). *Futures education: The world yearbook of education 1998*. London: Kogan Page.

Huitt, W. (1998). *Critical thinking: An overview* (Educational Psychology Interactive). Valdosta, GA: Valdosta State University. Retrieved November 6, 2007 from, http://chiron.valdosta.edu/whuitt/col/cogsys/critthnk.html

[Revision of paper presented at the Critical Thinking Conference sponsored by Gordon College, Barnesville, GA, March, 1993.]

Leistyna, P., Woodrum, A., & Sherblom, S. A. (1996). *Breaking free: The transformative power of critical pedagogy.* Cambridge, MA: Harvard Educational Review.

Mertes, L. (1991). Thinking and writing. *Middle School Journal, 22,* 24-25.

Noddings, N. (2003). *Caring: A feminine approach to ethics and moral education.* Berkeley, CA: University of California Press. (Original work published 1984)

Oxfam. (2006). *Education for global citizenship: A guide for schools.* Oxford, England: Oxfam.

Reardon, B. (1985). *Sexism and the war system.* New York: Teachers College Press.

Reardon, B. A. (2000). Peace education: A review and projection. In B. Moon, S. Brown, & M. B. Peretz (Eds.), *International companion to education* (pp. 21-34). New York: Routledge.

Rossatto, C. A. (2005). *Engaging Paulo Freire's pedagogy of possibility.* Oxford, England: Rowman & Littlefield.

Ruddick, M. (1989). *Maternal thinking: Toward a politics of peace.* Boston: Beacon Press.

Scriven, M., & Paul, R. (n.d.). *A working definition of critical thinking.* Retrieved November 6, 2007, from http://lonestar.texas.net/~mseifert/crit2.html

Stevens, C. (n.d.). *Critical pedagogy on the web.* Retrieved November 5, 2007, from http://mingo.info-science.uiowa.edu/~stevens/critped/terms.htm

United Nations. (1996). *Report of the United Nations High Commissioner for Human Rights on the implementation of the Plan of Action for the United Nations Decade for Human Rights.* Retrieved November 6, 2007, from http://www.unhchr.ch/huridocda/huridoca.nsf/(Symbol)/A.51.506.Add.1.En?OpenDocument

United Nations Educational, Scientific and Cultural Organization (1980). *World Congress on Disarmament Education: Report and final document.* Paris, France: UNESCO.

United Nations Educational, Scientific and Cultural Organization. (1999). *Declaration and programme of action on a culture of peace* (Resolution A/53/243). New York: United Nations General Assembly.

United States Agency for International Development (2002). *Approaches to civic education: Lessons learned.* Washington, DC: USAID.

Vagts, A. (1981). *A history of militarism.* (Rev. ed.). Westport, CT: Greenwood Press.

Wahlstrom, R. (1991, March). *Peace education meets the challenge of the cultures of militarism* (Peace Education Miniprints No. 11). Lund University, Sweden: Malmo School of Education.

FURTHER READING IN PEACE EDUCATION

Andreopoulos, G., & Claude, R, P (Ed.). (1997). *Human rights education for the twenty first century*. Philadelphia: University of Pennsylvania Press.

Assefa, H. (1993). *Peace and reconciliation as a paradigm: A philosophy of peace and its implications on conflict, governance, and economic growth in Africa*. Unpublished manuscript, Nairobi.

Bajaj, M. (2004). Human rights education and student self-conception in the Dominican Republic. *Journal of Peace Education, 1*(1), 21-34.

Bell, W. (Ed.). (1997). *Foundations of futures studies* (Vol. 2). New Brunswick, NJ: Transaction.

Bell, W. (1998). Understanding the futures field. In D. H. R. Slaughter (Ed.), *Futures education: The world yearbook of education* London: Kogan Page

Bell, W. (2004). The study of images of the future. In *Foundations of Futures Studies* (Vol. 1, pp. 81-86). New Brunswick, NJ: Transaction.

Bezold, C. (2005). The visioning method. In R. Slaughter (Ed.), *Knowledge base of futures studies* (Vol. 2). Brisbane: Foresight International.

Bonisch, A. (1981). Elements of the modern concept of peace. *Journal of Peace Research, 18*(2), 165-173.

Boulding, E. (1988). Uses of the imagination. In *Building a global civic culture*. New York: Teachers College Press

Boulding, E., & Boulding, K. (1995). *The future: Image and processes*. London: SAGE

Boulding, E. (1995). How children see their world and make their future. In E. Boulding & K. Boulding (Ed.), *The future: Image and processes*. London: SAGE.

Bretherton, D., Weston, J., & Zbar, V. (2003). Peace education in a post-conflict environment: The case of Sierra Leone. *Prospects, 33*(2), 219-230.

169

Brock-Utne, B. (1985). *Education for peace: A feminist perspective*. Willowdale, Ontario: Pergamon Press.

Brock-Utne, B. (1996). Peace education in post-colonial Africa. *Peabody Journal of Education, 71*(3), 170-190.

Burns, R., & Aspelagh, R. . (1996). *Three decades of peace education around the world*. New York: Garland.

Burns, R. J., & Aspelagh, R. (1983). Concepts of peace education: A view of western experience. *International Review of Education, 29*(3), 311-330.

Cardenas, S. (2005). Constructing rights? Human rights education and the state. *International Political Science Review, 26*(4), 363-379.

Curti, M. (1985). Reflections on the genesis and growth of peace history. *Peace and Change, X*, 1-18.

Danesh, H. B. (2006). Towards an integrative theory of peace education. *Journal of Peace Education, 3*(1), 55-78.

Dauncey, G. (1999). *Earth future: Stories from a sustainable world*. Gabriola, BC: New Society.

Davies, L. (2005). Schools and war: Urgent agendas for comparative & international education. *Compare, 35*(4), 357-371.

DeBenedetti, C. (1984). Peace history in the American manner. *The History Teacher, 18*(1), 75-115.

Editors. (2002). Special issue on human rights education. *International Review of Education, 48*(3-4).

Editors. (2005). Special issue on human rights education and transformational learning. *Intercultural Education, 16*(2).

Editors. (2006). Special issue on International Perspectives on Human Rights Education. *Journal of Social Science Education*. Retrieved from http://www.jsse.org/2006-1/index.html

Fountain, S. (1999). *Peace education in UNICEF*. New York: United Nations Children's Fund.

Galtung, J. (1969). Violence, peace, and peace research. *Journal of Peace Research, 6*(3), 167-191.

Galtung, J. (1985). Twenty-five years of peace research: Ten challenges and some responses. . *Journal of Peace Research, 22*(2), 141-158.

Galtung, J. (1990). Cultural violence. *Journal of Peace Research, 27*(3), 291-305.

Gerber, P. (2004). Black rights/white curriculum: Human rights education for indigenous peoples. *Deakin Law Review, 9*(1), 61-89.

Gur Ze'ev, I. (2001). Philosophy of peace education in a postmodern era. *Educational Theory, 51*(3), 315-336.

Haavelrsud, M. (1993). *Disarming: Discourse on violence and peace*. Norway: Arena.

Haavelsrud, M. (1996). *Education in developments*. Norway: Arena.

Hagglund, S. (1996). Developing concepts of peace and war: Aspects of gender and culture. *Peabody Journal of Education, 71*(3), 29-41.

Harber, C. (1996). Educational violence and education for peace in Africa. *Peabody Journal of Education, 71*(3), 151-169.

Harris, I., & Morrison, M. (2003). *Peace education*. New York: McFarland.

Harris, I. (2004). Peace education theory. *Journal of Peace Education, 1*(1), 5-20.

Hicks, D. (2002). Developing a futures dimension in the school curriculum. *Development Education Journal, 9*(1).

Howlett, C. (1982). The pragmatist as pacifist: John Dewey's views on peace education. *Teachers College Record, 83*(3), 435-452.

Jones, T. (2006). Combining conflict resolution education and human rights education: Thoughts for school-based peace education. *Journal of Peace Education, 3*(2), 187-208.

Kant, I. (1795). Perpetual peace: A philosophical sketch. In H. Reiss (Ed.), *Kant's political writings* (pp. 85-135). Cambridge: Cambridge Unviersity Press.

Killingsworth, R. S. (2005). Promoting a peaceful classroom through poetry. *Journal of Peace Education, 2*(1), 69-78.

Lauren, P. G. (2000). *The evolution of international human rights*. Philadelphia: University of Pennsylvania Press.

Lenhart, V., & Savolainen, K. (2002). Human rights education as a field of practice and theoretical reflection. *International Review of Education, 48*(3-4), 145-158.

McGynn, C., & Bekerman, Z. (2007). *Addressing ethnic conflict through peace education*. New York: Palgrave.

Montgomery, K. (2006). Racialized hegemony and nationalist mythologies: Representations of war and peace in high school history textbooks, 1945-2005. *Journal of Peace Education, 3*(1), 19-37.

Noddings, N. (2005). *Educating citizens for global awareness*. New York: Teachers College Press.

Ohanyan, A., & Lewis, J. (2005). Politics of peace-building: Critical evaluation of interethnic contact peace education in Georgian-peace camp, 1998–2002. *Peace and Change, 30*(1), 57-84.

Osler, A., & Vincent, K (2002). *Citizenship and the challenge of global education* Trentham Books.

Osseiran, S., & Reardon, B. (1998). The United Nation's role in peace education. In C. Alger (Ed.), *The future of the United Nations system: Potential for the twenty-first century* (pp. 385-408). New York: United Nations University Press.

Page, J. (2004). Peace education: Exploring some philosophical foundations. *International Review of Education, 50*(1), 3-15.

Prasad, S. N. (1998). Development of peace education in India (since independence). *Peace Education Mini Prints, 95*, 1-14.

Reardon, B. (1988). *Comprehensive peace education*. New York: Teachers College Press.

Reardon, B. (1993). *Women and peace: feminist visions of global security*. New York: State University of New York Press.

Reardon, B. (2000). Peace education: Review and projection. In B. Moon, M. Ben-peretz, & S. Brown (Ed.), *International companion to education*. New York: Routledge.

Reardon, B. (2001). *Education for a culture of peace in a gender perspective*. Paris, France: UNESCO.

Rivage-Seul, M. (1987). Peace education: Imagination and the pedagogy of the oppressed. *Harvard Educational Review, 57*(2), 153-170.

Salomon, G., & Nevo, B. (2002). *Peace education: the concept, principles, and practices around the world*. New Jersey and London: Erlbaum.

Sinclair, M. (2004). *Learning to live together*. Paris: UNESCO.

Sommers, M. (2004). *Peace education and refugee youth. Learning for a future: Refugee education in developing countries*. Geneva: UNHCR.

Suarez, D., & Ramirez, F. (2004). *Human rights and citizenship: The emergence of human rights education* Stanford, CA: Center on Democracy, Development and the Rule of Law.

Synott, J. (1996). Australian aboriginal constructions of humans, society, and nature in relation to peace education. *Peabody Journal of Education, 71*(3), 84-94.

Synott, J. (2005). Peace education as an educational paradigm: review of a changing field using an old measure. *Journal of Peace Education, 2*(1), 3-16.

Tandon, Y. (1989). *Militarism and peace education in Africa: A guide and manual for peace education and action in Africa*. Nairobi: African Association for Literacy and Adult Education.

Tarrow, N. (1992). Human rights education: Alternative conceptions. In J. Lynch, C. Modgil, & S. Modgil (Ed.), *Human rights, education and global responsibilities* (pp. 21-50): Falmer Press.

Thelin, B. (1996). Early tendencies of peace education in Sweden. *Peabody Journal of Education, 71*(3), 95-110.

Tibbits, F. (2002). Understanding what we do: Emerging models for human rights education. *International Review of Education, 48*(3-4), 159-171.

UNESCO. (2000). *World directory of peace research and training institutions*. Paris: UNESCO.

Vasquez, J. A. (1976). Toward a unified strategy for peace education: Resolving the two cultures problem in the classroom. *The Journal of Conflict Resolution, 20*(4), 707-728.

Vongalis-Macrow, A. (2006). Rebuilding regimes or rebuilding community? Teachers' agency for social reconstruction in Iraq. *Journal of Peace Education, 3*(1), 99-113.

Weber, T. (2001). Gandhian philosophy, conflict resolution theory and practical approaches to negotiation. *Journal of Peace Research, 38*(4), 493-513.

White, C., & Openshaw, R (Ed.). (2005). *Democracy at the crossroads: International perspectives on global citizenship education*. US: Lexington.

Wiberg, H. (1981). JPR 1964-1980: What have we learnt about peace? . *Journal of Peace Research, 18*(2), 111-148.

Wintersteiner, W. (1999). *Pedagogy of the other: Building blocks for peace education in the postmodern world*. Munster, Ireland: Agenda.

Wintersteiner, W. (2003). The "old Europe" and the new tasks for peace education. *Journal of Peace Education, 1*(1), 89-102.

Wittner, L. S. (1987). Peace movements and foreign policy: The challenge to diplomatic historians. *Diplomatic History, XI*, 355-370.

Wulf, C. (1974). *Handbook of peace education*. Frankfurt, Germany: International Peace Research Association.

INDEX

173

CPSIA information can be obtained at www.ICGtesting.com
Printed in the USA
LVOW070036270812

296054LV00001B/49/P